WATCHER ON THE HILLS

WATCHER
ON THE HILLS

by

RAYNOR C. JOHNSON
M.A. (Oxon), Ph.D., D.Sc. (Lond)
Master of Queen's College, University of Melbourne

"I believe the only news of any interest
does not come from the great cities or
from the councils of state, but from
some lonely watcher on the hills who
has a momentary glimpse of infinitude
and feels the universe rushing at him."
A. E.'S LETTERS TO MÍNANLÁBÁIN

HODDER AND STOUGHTON
LONDON SYDNEY AUCKLAND TORONTO

To MARY
with gratitude
and to our daughter
MAUREEN
with her father's affection

FOREWORD

by HILDA FRANCIS

"As above, so below." So it is that in the rhythms of growth in creatures around us, we find hints of the cycles of development in man and higher beings.

The trout is hatched in the source waters, and in the course of growth makes its way downstream to the sea. We have been living through a period of human development akin to these predominantly centrifugal activities. Our ideas and thoughts have become peripherally focussed into analytic and deductive patterns. All of us, especially scientists, explorers and inventors, have been working along the down-currents of our own specialities. This is a necessary phase of growth, for there is a two-fold circulation in us, as well as in the divine life. As we have grown in self-satisfaction we have had little vigour left to acquaint ourselves with our contemporaries' specialised knowledge, to estimate the overall increase of experience, or to remember that we derive our life and mind from one Source.

Dr. Raynor Johnson has not been happy with this centrifugal dissipation of energy, and has worked along other currents besides his own speciality of physics. He has realised further that it is no time to linger in the sea of separation when the dim scents of home-waters stir in the deeps of our being, calling us to begin a new phase of development and swim back towards our Source.

In his last two books, *The Imprisoned Splendour* and *Nurslings of Immortality*, he has been swimming in the right direction himself, and in this book he is pointing towards a meeting-place for seekers after truth both in East and West. His most potent directive is given in a footnote on page 113. He calls us to follow and see for ourselves a wider view of earthly and cosmic relationships, and perhaps even a glimpse of the Divine Humility which does not rest in majestic isolation above the sorrows and sins of men, but *leaps* through the cradle and the cross right down into the beings of His little creatures. This leaping down into our bodies and minds is the hidden impetus which gives us our present-day urge to turn and swim towards our Source—and the power to do it.

In this book Dr. Johnson has chosen thirty-six cases to illustrate the homeward swim of the human spirit. As the fish swims homewards, there are moments when we catch him standing up out of the water and breathing, as it were, a stronger air than when immersed in his watery element. He discovers another ocean—of air—and it is there whether he leaps into it or not. This seems to me a picture of the momentary contacts with higher levels of being of which many people tell in this book. Such contacts are helps and encouragements on the way, and they often occur for human beings at times of crisis. Then they discover that there is an ocean of Spirit—and nothing is ever repeated in this realm of boundless variety and beauty. Through the steady practice of the prayer of adoration and the life of self-giving we can have brief moments in these higher levels as we go along our earthly way.

Bigger leaps, however, are necessary in the upstream swim. Those who have watched trout leaping the weirs will appreciate this. Time and again the trout fall back into the mill-pond, till at last comes that amazing leap up—up above the weir to begin a new cycle of development. Their future destiny draws them like an unseen magnet and overcomes the downward pull of their previous cycle of growth. That moment gives them a fresh orientation to Reality. Such a moment in the history of mankind's development seems to be upon us now. *Watcher on the Hills* is one of the signs that such a leap is taking place in man's mind today. It seems to me a call to be heeded both by those to whom the data which Dr. Johnson has gleaned and sifted are fresh ground, and by those Christians who are dozing while dormant faculties lie undeveloped within them. Both will receive some surprises (perhaps shocks), and both will need to get rid of juvenile ideas and gain personal experience, here and now, of the realms of the *whole* Spirit. We are living in a time when great tidal waves of the Spirit carry ordinary men and women over the river-bars, so that many (instead of a few spiritual geniuses) are now given the opportunity to swim upstream. It is to these this book is addressed. These too can make the momentary "airy darts", called "acts of the will" by spiritual guides.

Even the top of the weir is not the end of the swim into maturity. It is a barrier to be surmounted before the creatures can enter into their fresh cycle of maturity on higher levels. The trout does not remain in the air after a leap, but submerges again into his ordinary element, becoming transformed *there*. So with mystics after such a leap. Dormant faculties then emerge, and there is an awakening and development of inner organs by which higher and higher levels of life and consciousness are contacted. Such degrees of enhanced consciousness and commitment are what we mean by "degrees of prayer", and lead us on into inter-relationships with higher and higher matrices of spiritual energy, which some mystics differentiate into hierarchies of spiritual beings. This gift of interaction with spiritual realms is not the goal of the mystic life. *The mystic seeks God,* not the thrills of personal experience which His touch through the various hierarchies brings him. Dr. Johnson realises this, and again and again reminds us of the lifelong discipline that contributes to the making of the man full-grown in Christ. The mature mystics are pioneers in these sudden mutations relating to enlargements of understanding and life. They balance securely above past and future, living richly in a creative "now".

The lack of mystical experience averred by the author is a noteworthy feature of this book. Some readers may question the value of his attempt. Others may appreciate their historic creeds all the more, after consideration of the difficulties with which he battles in trying to fit the mystic way into the concepts of Imaginism. (After all, concepts, even credal and philosophic ones, are only symbols when applied to these high levels of Being.)

Dr. Johnson is not trying to direct upstream swimmers, but disclosing the fact to those who are floundering in the deep whirlpool of modern frustration that these swimmers do find a life of joy.

One hears of gifted folk playing a welcoming tune to bring home the fishes. I hope Dr. Johnson will forgive my saying so, but his lovely swan-song in Chapter 11 is something like that, and I shall look forward to hearing more. Some things are beyond our understanding, but one does feel that this will weave its way into the crannies of divided minds and give them a right directive in reintegration. Our hearts may pull in the right direction, but as long as our minds are dispersed elsewhere our wills may be too weak to propel us on the long swim to our Source. But as we move, we find we have a Divine Companion, who is not far from each one of us.

Pant,
Oswestry,
Shropshire.

AUTHOR'S PREFACE

I HAVE written a book about mysticism, but this term is so misused and misunderstood that I have not dared to use it in the title. Many people suppose that this subject has vaguely to do with the mysterious, if not with mystification itself! Some imagine that it comprises the study of everything beyond the range of our five senses, including all psychical phenomena. Others who have some slight acquaintance with its extensive literature may conclude that it is a kind of exalted experience associated with intense preoccupation with the religious life. Those medical men who know anything about it have a tendency to regard it as psychopathic—a phenomenon related to manic-depressive states of mind. It is not difficult to see how all these ideas have arisen, but I am convinced that they are far from presenting a true picture of mysticism.

I must confess at once that I am a physicist by training and that I have had no mystical experience. To the reader it may seem strange that I should want to write a book on a subject which is clearly far removed from that of atoms and molecules with which I was initially trained to deal. The field is one which has been covered by the writings of theologians, philosophers, psychologists and general religious thinkers. Evelyn Underhill's well-known book, *Mysticism*, has a bibliography which shows the breadth of interest in this theme. I have no qualifications nor have I any desire to add to the large number of books which have made this kind of approach. But I must be truthful and say that while many of them are models of scholarship, devotion and piety, I doubt whether more than a few will ever be read by ordinary thoughtful intelligent people who are deeply concerned to find the truth about life. The language is often fervently religious, the framework theological, and the general effect is not likely to convey to the ordinary reader who dips into them that he has to do with something intimately related to his life. My approach is quite a different one, and I hope my readers will find it relevant to the business of living and helpful in their search for truth.

We live in an age which rightly asks for evidence: the scientific outlook has penetrated in some degree into Everyman's thinking. We do not live in an age of faith. When modern man thinks about the ultimate questions he is not disposed to accept ancient beliefs, he is not impressed by dogmatic assertion, and he is not able or prepared to respond to sweeping demands for "faith". To those who offer him views about the world, about human life and destiny, he asks, "What is your evidence?" One reason why I have written this book is to show how absurd it is to suppose that the only evidence to be weighed is that which our five senses provide. The human mind, which in all of us daily receives and interprets the evidence of the senses, also receives from time to time intimations, insights, moments of illumination, and occasionally vivid experiences, which are felt to be of the greatest significance by the percipient. This is evidence which has to be weighed carefully if we are in earnest to understand the world. I am not now thinking of psychical phenomena, but of experiences of a much deeper kind which can be differentiated from them.

I have already indicated that I shall make little or no reference to the great "classical" mystics, since they have been the subject of many books. Furthermore, as men and women of devout religious practices, it may well be said that in differing measure they found what they were seeking, and expressed it according to their own religious preconceptions. In the present book my judgments are based largely upon the experiences of ordinary people living in our midst and, because of this, they have for my purpose greater value. I have for some time been collecting and studying these accounts. When they are sifted carefully in order to set aside the merely psychical perception of other planes of being, visions which are symbolic representations of truth, and what we may call the data of inspiration, there is a solid core of testimony which satisfies the criteria for true mystical experience. I have found this enormously impressive. Here we seem to have evidence of Reality breaking through the screen of appearances: surely an occurrence of the deepest interest to every seeker after truth in every field. Where it happens, it brings with it an ecstasy of Joy, an unconditioned Certainty, and the knowledge that what IS is better than our highest hopes and most far-flung desires.

Perhaps I may help my reader by outlining the pattern of development in the book.

When man studied the outer world he devised innumerable instruments to supplement his limited senses. In the study of the inner world he is in a peculiar position for he is both the knower and the instrument of his own knowledge. It was inevitable, therefore, that the structure of man himself should be the subject matter of Chapter 2. I have not dealt in any detail with man's mind since this complex group of levels is not essentially involved in mystical experience. It is of course involved in expressing and interpreting it afterwards, but this is another matter. To attempt some understanding of mystical experience, I have thought a good deal about man's higher affiliations, i.e. with beings who operate consciously on higher significant levels of the world. These suggestions came in the first place through automatic scripts. They are not less worthy of consideration on that account, for where does man's inspiration in any field of enquiry come from? A thirsty man who is offered water is not concerned whether it is obtained from a tap, drawn from a well, or taken from a spring: it makes possible for him the next stage of his journey. The higher relationships of man seem to me to offer clues to the chief types of mystical experience, as we should expect them to do in a social universe. Chapter 2 is offered as a framework of ideas in the hope that it will illuminate a little the accounts which follow in Chapters 3 to 7. In Chapter 8 I have tried to show the relationship of the accounts of mystical experience given by ordinary people to the stages of the mystic way as expounded by the great Masters. Here I have also discussed the relationship of mysticism with religion and occultism. In Chapter 9 I have dealt with the modern concept of an "unconscious" mind, in order to rebut what I believe to be certain mistaken ideas which have a wide currency. It is a little technical, but I hope it will present no insurmountable difficulty to the non-specialist. In Chapter 10 I have briefly referred to various methods of expanding awareness, and discussed how far mystical experience may be regarded as induced. This is a matter of some interest at present when experiments are being made with mescalin and lysergic acid diethylamide (LSD). In the closing chapter I have endeavoured to relate mysticism to the ordinary person's life.

QUEEN'S COLLEGE,   RAYNOR C. JOHNSON.
UNIVERSITY OF MELBOURNE.

CONTENTS

CONTENTS

ACKNOWLEDGMENTS

I DESIRE to thank the following authors, publishers, and owners of copyright, for permission to quote extracts from the works mentioned below.

Messrs. George Allen & Unwin Ltd. for two extracts from *Letters to a Friend* by C. F. Andrews; the Editor of *Art Digest Inc.* for an extract from an article called *A John Ferren Profile* by J. Fitzsimmons; Messrs. Geoffrey Bles Ltd. for quotations from *Surprised by Joy* by C. S. Lewis; Messrs. Jonathan Cape Ltd. for a quotation from *Diagnosis of Man* by Kenneth Walker; Cambridge University Press Ltd. for a sentence from *McTaggart* by G. Lowes Dickinson; A. D. Peters for an extract from *The Invisible Writing* by Arthur Koestler published by Messrs. William Collins, Sons & Co. Ltd.; The C. W. Daniel Co. Ltd. for several quotations from *Recorded Illuminates* by Winslow Hall, M.D.; Messrs. Faber & Faber Ltd. for extracts from *The Geeta* as translated by Sri Purohit Swami; John Farquharson Esq. for a quotation from *Varieties of Religious Experience* by William James, and also from *The Wind and the Rain* by Thomas Burke published by Messrs. Thornton Butterworth & Co. Ltd.; Messrs L. N. Fowler & Co. Ltd. for an extract from *This Wondrous Way of Life* by Brother Mandus; Messrs. Victor Gollancz Ltd. for quotations from *A Drug-Taker's Notes* by R. H. Ward, and also from *The Woman Who Could Not Die* by Julia de Beausobre; Messrs. William Heinemann Ltd. for a quotation from *Saints and Revolutionaries* by Olaf Stapledon, and for a poem from *The Carved Stone* by Sir George Rostrevor Hamilton; Messrs. Christopher Johnson Ltd. for quotations from *Adventure into the Unconscious* by John Custance; Sir Francis Meynell and Messrs. Burns Oates & Washbourne Ltd. for two verses from *The Works of Francis Thompson*; Mr. Diarmuid Russell and Messrs. Macmillan & Co. Ltd. for several quotations from *The Collected Poems of A. E.*, and from *Song and its Fountains*; Messrs. Methuen & Co. Ltd. for several quotations from *Mysticism* by Evelyn Underhill; Messrs. John Murray Ltd. for an extract from *Heart of Nature* by Sir Francis Younghusband; Oxford University Press for quotations from *Eastern Religions and Western Thought* by S. Radhakrishnan, and from *Mysticism, Sacred and Profane* by R. C. Zaehner; Messrs. Rider & Co. Ltd. for quotations from *An Introduction to Zen Buddhism* by D. T. Suzuki (one being from C. G. Jung's Foreword and a quotation of Professor Nukariya); Messrs. Routledge & Kegan Paul Ltd. for quotations from *Between Man and Man* by Martin Buber, from *The Integration of the Personality* by C. G. Jung and from C. G. Jung's Psychological Commentary in W. Y. Evans-Wentz' book *The Tibetan Book of the Great Liberation*; Messrs. Sidgwick & Jackson Ltd. for the last fifteen lines of Rupert Brooke's poem *The Song of the Pilgrims* from *The*

Complete Poems of Rupert Brooke; J. M. Watkins Esq. for an extract from *The Golden Fountain*; Messrs. A. P. Watt & Son and Mrs. W. B. Yeats for the last verse of the poem *The Lake Isle of Innisfree* taken from *Collected Poems of W. B. Yeats* published by Messrs. Macmillan & Co. Ltd.; The Editor of *The Atlantic Monthly* for quotations from an article of Margaret Montague entitled *Twenty Minutes of Reality*; Messrs. E. P. Dutton & Co. Inc. for a passage from *Cosmic Consciousness* by R. M. Bucke.

In writing a book such as this, I have a particular indebtedness to all those persons who have generously shared with me their inner experiences, and whose anonymity I undertook to preserve. I wish to take this opportunity of thanking them—both those whose accounts I have used in the text, and those whose accounts I was not able to use. I desire to thank very warmly Dr. Crookall and Major W. Tudor Pole, who both placed at my disposal their own gathered collections of material.

I wish to express my special thanks to Mr. John Redwood-Anderson, the English poet, not only for allowing me to quote some of his poetry and prose, but for the insights and the philosophical outlook of his fine mind which he has generously shared with me in personal correspondence.

Finally, I wish to acknowledge a particular debt to Miss Hilda Francis, who has honoured me by writing a Foreword to this book. She has been a kindly and very helpful critic of the book, and has enriched it at many points by her own experience of the world Within and Beyond.

RAYNOR C. JOHNSON.

Chapter

I

INTRODUCTION

> We cannot reach the meaning or higher significance of anything by
> any unaided logical process, but only by an illumination of the whole
> personality which lifts it to new basic conceptions . . . We cannot deal
> with the world as it is in itself, but only with the world as it is for us . . .
> The point which stands out clearly is that the meaning of a thing depends,
> not on the thing itself, but also on the extent to which one's personality
> can respond to it . . . In our view the boundary which restricts our
> knowledge of the real is in ourselves. It is a subjective boundary.
>
> G. N. M. TYRRELL

GRADES OF SIGNIFICANCE

IN a book with this title which deserves to be closely studied by all
who are concerned with the search for truth, G. N. M. Tyrrell[1] has
reminded us that the significance which men attach to anything
depends on the presuppositions (often scarcely recognised) with
which they view it. A mountain peak may be to a surveyor a difficult
terrain to be surveyed, to a climber a challenge to his mountaineering
skill, to a farmer a trustworthy sign of rain, and to an artist a drama
of form, light and shade. All these views are right but limited. None
of them are more than partial aspects of what the mountain is in its
completeness. In this instance, most of us would rank the artist's
view as of higher significant value than the others. Sometimes the
differences in value of various viewpoints are particularly significant.
Tyrrell has pointed out that a book seen by a dog may be merely a
coloured shape. An intelligent savage who had never seen a book
before might be curious about the multitude of black symbols on
the white paper. By close analysis of them he might discover an
alphabet, the principles of word construction, and grammar. To an
educated man the same book would be full of meanings. We can
imagine these two men discussing the book. The savage might
maintain that the letters, words and laws of grammar embodied its
complete significance, and that it was merely fanciful to suppose that
it contained anything more. The educated man might maintain
without avail that the book embodied meanings of which the words
were only symbols. The same object has been viewed on three

[1] *Grades of Significance* (Rider & Co. Ltd., 2nd Ed. 1947)

different levels of significance and each viewpoint proved incomprehensible to those on a lower level.

Where man himself is the object of study, he may be regarded on the lowest level as a complex physico-chemical machine, on the biologist's level as a living organism of a successful species, on the psychologist's level as a self-determining being with great capacity for thinking and feeling, and on the sage's level as "a god, though in the germ". By and large, Western thought has reached the point of looking at man as a participant in two levels—body and mind (this latter being complex)—but recognises no levels higher and more significant than mind. The so-called unconscious levels of mind have become a convenient repository of those faculties and powers which do not fit into this two-level theory of being.

When a poet wrote:[1]

> And nothing's truly seen that's mean:
> Be it a sand, an acorn, or a bean,
>   It must be cloth'd with endless glory,
>   Before its perfect story
>   (Be the spirit ne'er so clear)
>   Can in its causes and its ends appear . . .

all the mystics would endorse his view. Yet, on the whole, it is true that Western thinkers would regard such a claim as fanciful and characteristic of poetic licence. It was this accusation of being fanciful and incomprehensible which the savage made against the educated man in regard to the book. It is an attitude generally adopted towards those who perceive on a higher level of significance by those who perceive on a lower.

In this book we shall be studying some of the highest experiences of mankind—experiences not easy to express in words, but embodying insights and feelings far beyond those normally present to ordinary people. In our opinion, some of these are clear indications of the existence of levels in man higher than those of mind—levels in which we are all doubtless immersed, but to which as yet only a few seem qualified to make a conscious response. We should not be surprised at this. The book (in our illustration) may seem to one man dull and unimportant, while to another it may unfold vistas of knowledge and truth. In the same way, poetry, music and art are assessed differently according to the quality of the personality brought to them. The limiting factor is within the observing subject.

[1] Thomas Traherne, *Poems*, p. 84 (Bertram Dobell, London, 1906)

EXAMPLES OF MYSTICAL EXPERIENCE

Before attempting to understand the nature of mystical experience we shall look at a few examples of it. Jacob Boehme, one of the most interesting mystics known to history (1575–1624), was a humble German shoemaker. It is recorded that once when quite young "he was surrounded by a divine light for seven days, and stood in the highest contemplation and Kingdom of Joy". At the age of twenty-five he had a second experience, apparently stimulated by gazing upon a burnished pewter dish. His biographer says:[1]

"He fell into an inward ecstasy, and it seemed to him as if he could now look into the principles and deepest foundations of things. He believed that it was only a fancy, and in order to banish it from his mind, he went out into the green. But here he remarked that he gazed into the very heart of things, the herbs and grass, and that actual nature harmonised with what he had inwardly seen. He said nothing of this to anyone, but praised and thanked God in silence."

About ten years later he had another experience which gave him a far-reaching Intellectual Illumination so that he could write:

"The gate was opened to me, that in one quarter of an hour I saw and knew more than if I had been many years together at a university, at which I exceedingly admired, and thereupon turned my praise to God for it. For I saw and knew the Being of all Beings, the Byss and the Abyss, and the Eternal Generation of the Holy Trinity, the Descent and Original of the World, and of all creatures through the Divine Wisdom: I knew and saw in myself all the three Worlds, namely the Divine, angelical and paradisical; and the dark World the Original of the Nature to the Fire; and then thirdly the external and visible World, being a Procreation or external Birth from both the internal and spiritual Worlds . . ."

Boehme's modes of expression are antiquated and in obvious need of interpretation. Similarly, the books which he felt impelled to write, humble and unlettered as he was, are full of the symbolism of alchemy and read strangely to modern eyes. It is clear, however, that this "inspired shoemaker" was struggling with such language and symbols as he knew to convey a little of the Reality which underlies appearances and which was so close to him throughout his life.

[1] Martensen, *Jacob Boehme*, p. 7

To a disciple who was anxious to know how to attain the same experience he could only say:

"Blessed art thou therefore if that thou canst stand still from self-thinking and self-willing, and canst stop the wheel of imagination and senses; forasmuch as hereby thou mayest arrive at length to see the great salvation of God, being made capable of all manner of Divine sensations and heavenly communications. Since it is nought indeed but thine own hearing and willing that do hinder thee, so that thou dost not see and hear God."

The next case I will mention is that of Dr. R. M. Bucke (1837–1902), a man whose early life had been full of adventurous activity, and who became one of the foremost Canadian psychiatrists. He was Superintendent of the Provincial Asylum for the Insane at Hamilton, Ontario, and was also Professor of Mental and Nervous Diseases at Western University. In his thirty-sixth year he had an experience which profoundly influenced his outlook on life and his subsequent researches. He relates[1] that he was in a peaceful frame of mind, travelling home in a hansom cab.

"All at once, without warning of any kind, he found himself wrapped around, as it were, by a flame-coloured cloud. For an instant he thought of fire—some sudden conflagration in the great city; the next he knew that the light was within himself. Directly afterwards there came upon him a sense of exultation, of immense joyousness, accompanied or immediately followed by an intellectual illumination quite impossible to describe. Into his brain streamed one momentary lightning-flash of the Brahmic splendour which has ever since lightened his life; upon his head fell one drop of Brahmic bliss, leaving thenceforward for always an after-taste of heaven . . . Like a flash there is presented to his consciousness a clear conception in outline of the meaning and drift of the universe. He does not come to believe merely; but he sees and knows that the cosmos, which to the self-conscious mind seems made up of dead matter, is in fact far otherwise—is in very truth a living presence . . . He sees that the life which is in man is eternal as all life is eternal; that the soul of man is immortal as God is; that the universe is so built and ordered that without any peradventure all things work together for the good of each and all; that the foundation principle of the world is what we call love, and that the happiness of every individual is in the long run absolutely certain . . . He claims that he learned more within the few seconds during which the illumination lasted than in previous months or even years of study, and that he learned much that no study could ever have taught . . . Its effect

[1] R. M. Bucke, *Cosmic Consciousness* (E. P. Dutton & Co.)

proved ineffaceable; it was impossible for him ever to forget what at that time he saw and knew; neither did he, nor could he, ever doubt the truth of what was then presented to his mind."

These two cases are characterised by intellectual illumination as well as supremely blissful emotion. Mystical experience does not necessarily include a flood of intellectual illumination at the time, as the following account shows. The lady Mrs. L. who, in middle life, wrote the account of her experience as a girl of 14, speaks (p. 56) of the legacy of knowledge which was left behind, on which she was able to draw as her understanding grew.

She relates that it took place at the age of fourteen when she was a regular attender at a Sunday School:

"I must have been a serious student, because as I approached adolescence, it seemed important that I find this God of whom I seemed to have a healthy picture. But finding God seemed a complex business, with few if any clues to start with. Apparently, if one loved enough one was sure to find God. But how did one go about loving? Love just happens. However, I tried and I did earnestly seek . . .

"It was a young people's meeting and, as I discovered later, an evangelical one. I had never heard of evangelism before, and can't say that I was particularly impressed. The speaker was fortunately not the blood-and-thunder type, but neither were his words particularly persuasive to me. Because the church was packed, I had a seat next to a doorway, and as the service was about to end, something impelled me to slip outside. It was a strange church and I did not know where the door led, so was a little bewildered by my act of faith. I have a vague memory of doors in all directions and finally of someone directing me upstairs. I didn't want to go upstairs, but not knowing where else to go, I went. I remember noting the dusty unwelcome appearance of the place as I climbed, until as I neared the top step something inexplicable happened. It was as though I had suddenly pushed up through the mists into a clear beautiful atmosphere. I neither saw nor heard. I just felt an indescribable ecstasy as I was suddenly conscious of an overwhelming love which seemed to encompass all that was and is and will be. It was all-encompassing and personal at the same time and lifted me to superb heights. I can remember feeling exultantly 'This is God', and God, after all, was both personal and immense. I wish I had at my command the words which would truly convey the power, the depth, the infinity, the gentleness, the serenity and the intimacy which intermingled then. Somehow one doesn't separate the qualities which were evident. One just wants to enjoy the Oneness of it all.

"I remember entering a room where were people I knew, but while I acknowledged their greeting, I was still lost in my new world. Perhaps because of my age, the memory remained so vivid that the moment seemed to be still with me. For days it seemed that I lived in that rarer atmosphere, yet still did my jobs with earnestness. In fact they seemed easy and interesting now. I seemed to be in two worlds at once and living both fully! But it was the new world that really held me. The experience seemed to affect my face somehow, because those who knew me used to remark on my face, and once when I was travelling in a train with two unknown passengers, I heard one whisper to the other, 'Hasn't that girl got a lovely face?' I was not a beauty.

"At the end of about a week while I was talking to my own minister it all suddenly disappeared. It seemed as though I was suddenly plunged back into darkness, and I was in despair. One doesn't easily let such an experience just vanish, so again I began to search, this time knowing what I was seeking. For months I searched and then gradually, very gradually, some of the Love returned (that full Love which is very hard to describe), and some of the understanding, but the ecstasy was gone. However, I found after a while, that if I were alone, preferably right out in the bush, I could sometimes recapture a little of the moment again, and I began to rebuild my life on the scraps which I recovered . . . but always I had that moment to recall and take courage from."

I shall include one more example which is the account of a young man, now a doctor:

"I was travelling back to camp in early January 1948 in an empty railway carriage after a short leave over Christmas from the army. I pulled *Diagnosis of Man* from my pack and began to read the chapter on Brahmanism. I was reading the words telling of the ever-present and all-pervading quality of Brahman, when suddenly my whole being was seized by an acute state of awareness, and immediately the words assumed a great significance. I knew somehow that they were true, that Brahman (at that time I suppose I translated it as God) *was* all about me, and through me, and in me. The knowledge did not come from without, unmistakably it came from within. The state was one of extraordinary joy; I realised happiness was within me. (I believe I also felt that I controlled great power, so that I could have stopped the train just by willing it, but in writing of this afterwards as I do, I cannot be certain of this.) I can remember looking out at the countryside passing by, and everything, the trees, meadows and hedges, were all part of me, and I of them, and all were in a great unity through which was God. Everything was a whole.

"The experience lasted a few minutes, and very gradually it ebbed away. But I *knew* with completely unshakable conviction that I had been in touch with Reality in those few minutes."

24

These four cases are not to be regarded as representative types of mystical experience, but simply as illustrations which may help to convey to the reader an impression of the data we shall have to deal with. We are only remarking at this stage that these persons were lifted up above their normal level of perception, so that they both felt and knew with a far wider and intenser appreciation. The experience was recognised by them as contact with a greater reality. A higher grade of significance disclosed itself, and they were participants in it.

SIGNIFICANCE FOR THE ORDINARY MAN

The ordinary person who reads of these things is probably not a little puzzled. He lives in a world which his senses disclose to him: he can see and hear and handle it. It is solid and substantial, and scientists seem to have mastered the laws of its behaviour.

He recognises another and far more variable world within man's soul—a world of feelings and thoughts, of imaginations and hopes and dreams and moral choices. It is not a world shared wholly in common, as is the outer world, but there are times when every man is made aware that it is nevertheless shared in some degree. Massed currents of fear, hatred and mistrust menace the integrity of the individual mind, and even threaten the physical existence of mankind. In such a world the ordinary man, when he thinks about it, feels bewildered. He craves very naturally for some security: some strong point to which he may cling when the storm beats upon him fiercely. He also longs to see meaning and purpose in the vast and often tragic pattern of human history, and not least in that present portion of it in which he, and those he loves, are immersed. The ordinary man has not the excitement of influencing events but the pain of suffering them. "The trivial round and common task" furnish him all too frequently with little inspiration and much anxiety.

It may be said that religion should meet these deeper needs: that it should proclaim the span of one lifetime as but a fragment of a long journey, that it should unfold meaning in his pilgrimage, and give him confidence to tread the way with a heart serene amid its challenges. But are there many men who have a religion which can do this for them? I do not think so. This religion of which I write is not a matter of professing certain beliefs, accepting a certain code of conduct, and attending religious services. It is a persistent orientation of the soul in love towards God, and the patient, humble treading of the path of self-forgetful service to one's fellows.

There are of course other counsels. Faced with the world as it is, certain great Eastern religions have advised their followers to withdraw from its delusions and futilities. "Men who love nothing in the world are rich in joy and free from pain", said the Buddha. But what if pain has something to teach us which we can learn in no other way? The lesson must be learned: escape is no solution. I am well aware that there are many paths to the Supreme, and that each man is free to choose. I am certainly not among those who proclaim but one Way. I can only say to Western man that if he will but tread it, there is a Way before him as clear and direct as that of any yogi or contemplative sitting in an Eastern cave or forest. The greatest of all mystics, Jesus Christ, knew the ordinary man well, and loved him—in the world. He saw the struggling goodness in most unlikely people. He appreciated the daily miracles of Nature. He was fond of children. The joy of life so radiated from Him that others were glad to be in His company. I shall say to my reader (and to myself), "Go thou, and do likewise."

But perhaps he will reply with sincere regret, "These things are what I should like to do, but cannot. They are doubtless the fruits of the mystic's attainment—but I have no mystical capacity. I have practically no sense of the existence of a world of Reality underlying the physical."

I have written this book to present evidence for such a world. The accounts which are given are not those of cloistered saints. Whether justifiably or not, it is always possible to suppose that the person who lives a life withdrawn from normal interests and centred upon religious matters may enjoy self-created bliss, and perhaps find what he has so long desired, because he has desired it. The accounts presented are of ordinary people like ourselves immersed in the world's life, with no such anticipation at the time of their visitation. They describe moments when their souls' eyes opened, as it were, and they saw and knew with complete and unshakable conviction the underlying nature of the world. These never-to-be-forgotten moments came to ordinary people, and in their testimony I find the deepest and most convincing assurance that "All is Well".

Chapter

2

MAN AND HIS HIGHER AFFILIATIONS

I pitied one whose tattered dress
Was patched, and stained with dust and rain;
He smiled on me; I could not guess
The viewless spirit's wide domain.

He said, "The royal robe I wear
Trails all along the fields of light:
Its silent blue and silver bear
For gems the starry dust of night.

The breath of Joy unceasingly
Waves to and fro its folds starlit,
And far beyond earth's misery
I live and breathe the joy of it."
                      A. E. (*The Vesture of the Soul*)

IN a B.B.C. talk William Golding[1] spoke of "the measureless gap
between the poetic perception of reality and prosaic unreal common-
sense". In another phrase he spoke of language which "fits over
experience like a strait-jacket". Of no theme could this be more
manifestly true than mysticism, for here, if anywhere, is immediacy
of experience. To present a structure of words in terms of which we
imagine we account for mysticism is like writing an anatomical
text-book to account for the beauty of a beautiful face. Language
must always be an inadequate vehicle of communication between
incarnate human beings. It cannot cope with either sensations or
feelings. Who can describe the taste of a strawberry to a person who
has not tasted one, or the ecstasy of loving to a person who has never
loved? How much less can language hope to convey the nature of
man's highest moments. It is primarily a device for facilitating the
processes of commonplace living, and the power of poets and great
writers to make language the vehicle of so much more is at least in
part due to *our* participation in levels which are not nourished by
the surface phenomena of life. The reader may feel, as I do, that
many of those whose accounts of mystical experience are presented
in subsequent chapters have used words very effectively to convey
something of a Reality which is beyond words. In this chapter our

---

[1] *Dear to My Heart*, a series of eight talks published by the B.B.C.

task is a prosaic one, and its subject-matter is frankly the anatomy of mysticism and not its countenance.

SOUL AND PERSONALITY

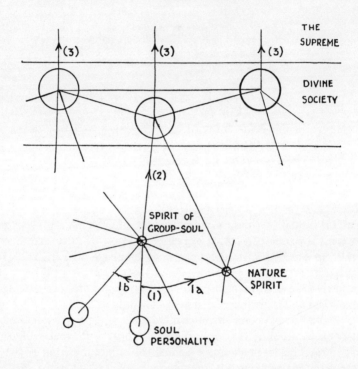

The diagram shown above may seem rather odd to some of my readers. Let me hasten to say that it is a simple and quite inadequate attempt to present the existence of a number of relationships. If it proves a hindrance rather than a help to the reader, he may ignore it. I have written elsewhere[1] on the structure of man on levels of soul and personality and it will be sufficient to deal very briefly with them here.

When a man speaks of himself, he probably thinks of a separate and distinct entity, with a sense of continuity achieved through his memory, comprising a distinctive group of desires, preferences, likes —

[1] *Nurslings of Immortality*, Chap. 9 (Hodder & Stoughton Ltd., 1957)

and dislikes, hopes, fears and ideals. He recognises that these may all be slowly modified (like his physical body), so that the man of sixty looks back on the man of twenty with some measure of amazement at the change. The entity which says *I* know, *I* feel, *I* hope, has an enduringness which he feels is above this flux of change. With this enduring "I" he associates his will and his consciousness. I don't think he feels this "I" is quite unchanging, but rather that its rate of change is vastly slower and concerned only with an inherent maturity, which is perhaps described as wisdom. This "I" I identify with a centre in the soul; it communicates with and through the personality at all times of sincerity of the latter. Its wisdom is usually available to the personality as intuition. Intuition is the distilled essence of past experience and it is substantially equivalent to wisdom. The soul possesses this treasure partly from its higher affiliations and partly from the personalities of past lives which it has put forth into incarnation.

The personality is the man as he is known to his contemporaries. It is that which he has built during his current life, and it is that which he will carry with him for a considerable time into the after-death life. As he advances after death to higher levels, his greater being—the soul—will express itself more completely, and will incorporate all the memories and experience of that particular personality which are worth preserving.

A. E. (George Russell), the Irish mystic and poet, who was a profound explorer of the soul, has left on record[1] some of his experiences:

"Looking back on the past I have a vivid sense of a being seeking incarnation here, beginning with those first faint intuitions of beauty, and those early dreamings which were its forerunners. It was no angelic thing, pure and new from a foundry of souls, which sought embodiment, but a being stained with the dust and conflict of a long travel through time, carrying with it unsated desires, base and august, and, as I divined of it, myriads of memories and a secret wisdom . . . There are two wisdoms in us, the wisdom we are born with and the wisdom we acquire."

THE HIGH SELF OR SPIRITUAL CENTRE

In the opinion of those who have explored most deeply, there is a Spirit beyond the soul. Various terms are used to describe it—the

---

[1] *Song and Its Fountains*, pp. 16, 52 (Macmillan & Co. Ltd., 1932)

High Self, the Oversoul, the Divine Spark, the true unmanifested "I". I shall quote A. E. again.[1]

"I am a far exile from that great glory, and can but peer through a dusky transparency to a greater light than the light of day. That greater light shines behind and through the psyche. It is the light of spirit which transcends the psyche as the psyche in its own world transcends the terrestrial ego. The psyche has a dual nature, for in part it is earth-bound, and in part it clings to the ancient spirit . . . While I could comprehend a little about the nature of the psyche, I could not apprehend at all the spirit which transcends the soul, for, as the seers said of it, it is eternal, invisible and universal . . . We cannot say that it is more within the heart than it is in air, or sunlight, rock or sea, or that it is more in heaven than earth. It is within us and without us. When we love we are really seeking for it, and I think our most passionate kisses are given to that Lover who will not surrender to us. It cannot be constrained. But there are enchanted hours when it seems to be nigh us, nigher to us than the most exquisite sweetness in our transitory lives."

In Christian teaching no clear distinction is made between soul and personality, presumably because the need for it only becomes apparent when reincarnation is recognised. A distinction is, however, made by St. Paul and others between soul (psyche) and spirit (pneuma).

The Buddha, whose teaching has frequently been misunderstood in the West, denied the permanence of the personality (with which most men identify themselves), but most definitely affirmed the High Self or Spirit. He said little about the individual soul, but implicitly recognised it when he gave it the advice, "Be such as have the Self as your lamp, Self as only refuge." "For one who has attained there is nought dearer than the Self." He was not prepared to discuss Nirvana, but it seems probable that it is just this attainment of the High Self that it refers to. The extinction or literally "blowing out", which term Nirvana means, refers to the transformation of the finite soul which disappears in Enlightenment into the great Self.

Hindu thought also makes a sharp distinction between the finite self in space and time, and the one true Self (the Atman) which is said to be the same in all and not divisible. The highest affirmation of Hinduism is that the Atman and the Brahman (the Supreme Being) are identical. The recognition of a lower and a higher self is expressed picturesquely in the Mundaka Upanishad: "Two birds, fast-bound companions, clasp close the self-same tree. Of those two,

[1] *loc. cit.*, pp. 112–14. A. E. uses the term *psyche* for *soul*.

one eats sweet fruit; the other looks on without eating." Strictly speaking, Hinduism would affirm that it is only illusion (maya) which leads us to recognise *two* birds: the first is illusory while the second alone is real!

There appears on the surface to be a difference of viewpoint between Christianity on the one hand, and Hinduism and Buddhism on the other. Christianity lays emphasis on the value of the individual soul as being dear to God.[1] Hinduism and Buddhism ascribe no final reality to the soul, but only to the One Self manifest in all. Defenders of the first would say that to them it is incredible that the whole process of evolution could produce such noble souls as were obviously manifested through the personalities of Gautama, Lao-Tse, Socrates and St. Francis, only that their distinctiveness as finite centres—observing or observed—should be *lost* in the One. Why all the travail of aeons of time? Why, indeed, the process of becoming? Is it *only* for the expansion of the One? If this is seriously maintained—that there is only one Reality—then the world in which many seem to exist must be an illusion or unreal. On the other hand the defenders of Hinduism and Buddhism who defend the One Reality from which all things proceed, by which they are sustained, and to which they return, are in the strongest of all philosophical positions, provided Reality is not merely contrasted with unreality, but is recognised as existing in different degrees.

I do not think these two apparently conflicting viewpoints are really at variance at all. One is stressing the "form" aspect of existence and the other is stressing its essential nature. One is stressing the idea of the Many, and the other is stressing the idea of the One. I shall not pursue this theme further at this stage; it is dealt with in Chapter 8. The truth, I believe, rests not in the recognition of a One *and* a Many, but in the recognition of a One-Many. This profound truth is reflected on many levels of the world, and when we rise above the physical level we must be prepared to encounter great Beings who are at the same time One and Many—to whom the term a One-Many can rightly be applied.

GROUP-SOULS

In the diagram I have represented spiritual centres to which souls are united as expressions of the one Spirit. Here we have one example of a Group-being or a One-Many. It might be described as a fellowship if this word were given much deeper content than

---

[1] Matt. x. 29, 31; Luke xii. 6, 7 etc.

in ordinary use, where it is synonymous with a free association of individuals having a community of interests. Here, the relationship is organic, and the souls are created and nourished by the one central sustaining spirit of the Group. If the reader asks what evidence there is for such Group-beings, I shall refer him to communications which I believe to come from F. W. H. Myers through the sensitive Miss G. Cummins.[1] I quote below two passages which I think provide a guide to right thinking in this field:

"A spirit . . . which nourishes a number of journeying souls with its light is a thought of God. This thought is individual in that it has a certain apartness from its Creator, the apartness of the created thing from the One who gave it birth . . . These myriad thoughts, or spirits, differ from one another; many of them, nearly all, before they control and manifest themselves in matter, are crude, innocent and incomplete embryos. They must gather to themselves numberless experiences, manifest and express themselves in uncountable forms before they attain to completion, before they may know perfect wisdom, true reality."

"A spirit manifests itself many times on earth, and it is the bond which holds together a number of souls who, in the ascending scale of psychic evolution, act and react upon one another. So when I talk of my spiritual forebears I do not speak of my physical ancestors, I speak of those soul-ancestors who are bound to me by one spirit. There may be contained within that spirit twenty souls, a hundred souls, a thousand souls. The number varies."

I have confidence in these scripts, for reasons which I have discussed elsewhere. A communication which came to me from another source has strengthened my belief in the conception of the Group-soul. My communicator said:

"The souls of human beings travel in groups, and members of each group are inter-related and make a pattern. Discarnate and incarnate souls belong to a group. Though individualised on the earth-plane and seemingly isolated units, on the deeper level they share a common unconscious. In this sphere I am a member of the Group-soul to which belong [names mentioned], and in its higher centres certain mystics. These latter are no longer concerned with the world of men. But those I have mentioned are still passionately concerned with it. On the incarnate level you [names mentioned] and others belong to this Group-soul. When the time is ripe there has to be a move forward in the design or pattern."

The Spirit which nourishes a Group is finite, but possesses great wisdom and knowledge. To its original treasury, potential or actual, it has added much that its member-souls have gathered through

[1] Geraldine Cummins, *The Road to Immortality* (Aquarian Press Ltd., 1956)

ages of time. Perhaps it is true to say that it has actualised potential knowledge which its souls have awakened through their experiences. When all the related souls have reached a certain high level of development the Group is a mighty being, a minor god, a mature One-Many, which can take its place in the Divine Society which governs our world-system. It is interesting to notice that A. E. supports this by his statement, "I have no doubt there are beings as far transcending us in wisdom and power as we may transcend the amoeba."[1]

Few of us ever speculate upon man's higher affiliations, probably for the good reason that our knowledge in this field is exceedingly meagre. Furthermore, it is only when we begin to think about mystical experience that we are driven to consider such possibilities. The religious outlook, naturally enough, has to be related to every-day living, and it therefore easily makes the assumption that man— this aspiring little creature on a wayside planet—is the crown of creation, and of peculiar, if not unique, interest to the Maker of endless galaxies. The mystic, when he philosophises, is driven towards a broader view in which the universe is seen as a living hierarchy, sustained and nourished by the Supreme Imagination. Its divine life flows outward through innumerable great beings and lesser ones, finally reaching to the smallest and remotest sentient "particles". This divine life is flowing forth, to return again ultimately to its Source in fully-conscious, perfect beings, beyond our highest conception.

MYSTICAL EXPERIENCE

We are now in a position to consider our main theme. How is mystical experience in its many forms to be regarded? Can it be related to the concepts we have outlined? I will state here my basic proposition: that *the primary and fundamental type of mystical experience is union of the soul with its Spirit* (symbolised by (1) in the diagram).

I think this is generally recognised by those who have given thought to the subject. Evelyn Underhill,[2] speaking of the spiritual self as "this immortal spark from the central fire", says, "The mystic way must therefore be a life, a discipline, which will so alter the constituents of his mental life as to include this spark within the conscious field." Again, she says, "The object of the mystic's adven-

---

[1] *loc. cit.*, p. 120
[2] Evelyn Underhill, *Mysticism*, pp. 55, 68 (Methuen & Co. Ltd., 1949 Ed.)

ture, seen from within, is the apprehension of, or direct communion with that transcendental Reality . . . The surface must co-operate with the deeps and at last merge with those deeps to produce that unification of consciousness upon high levels that alone can put a term to man's unrest."

Turning to the Indian philosopher Radhakrishnan,[1] we find this same truth frequently stated in his writings.

"The transcendent self stoops down, as it were, and touches the eyes of the empirical self overwhelmed by the delusion of the world's work. When the individual withdraws his soul from all outward events, gathers himself together inwardly and strives with concentration, there breaks upon him an experience, secret, strange and wondrous, which quickens within him, lays hold on him and becomes his very being." (p. 22)

"The highest wisdom is to know the Self . . . The Self is more than the ego; personality is truly a mask. The Self is the silent eternal witness, a light that no power can extinguish, whose attributes are truth and beauty, peace and wisdom, our true being which we do not perceive on account of the cloud of ignorance which covers our eyes . . . This spiritual consciousness is not a metaphysical fantasy but one that can be realised by each of us. In this transcendental consciousness, where the body is still, the mind attains quiescence, and thought comes to rest, we are in contact with the pure spirit of which the states of waking, dream, and sleep are imperfect articulations." (p. 123)

"These memorable moments of our life reveal to us the truth that we are, though we soon lapse from them into the familiar life of body, sense and mind; and yet these moments of our divine existence continue to guide us the rest of our lives as 'pillars of cloud by day, pillars of fire by night'. The soul is led through a succession of states until in the depths of its own being it experiences the touch of divinity and feels the life of God. By breaking through the entanglements of created things, the veils of sense and of intellect, the soul establishes itself in the nudity of spirit. The seer no longer distinguishes himself from that which is seen. He is one with the centre which is the centre of all . . . God ceases to be an object external to the individual and becomes a consuming experience." (pp. 129-30)

One of the clearest indications of the nature of the basic mystical experience is found in the form of yoga advocated by the great Indian saint Sri Ramana Maharishi who died in 1950. In a recent book Mouni Sadhu,[2] one of his European disciples, who practised this yoga of the "Direct Path", tells of moments of mystical illumina-

[1] S. Radhakrishnan, *Eastern Religions and Western Thought* (O.U.P., 1939)
[2] Mouni Sadhu, *In Days of Great Peace* (George Allen & Unwin Ltd.)

34

tion which he experienced. Most impressive, however, is his account of the spiritual atmosphere around the Maharshi's saintly figure—for he was recognised as one who dwelt in, and could maintain at will, this illuminated state. His instructions to those who would follow his path were simple:

"Pursue the enquiry 'Who am I?' relentlessly. Analyse your entire personality. Try to find out where the I-thought begins. Go on with your meditations. Keep turning your attention within. One day the wheel of thought will slow down and an intuition will mysteriously arise. Follow that intuition, let your thinking stop, and it will eventually lead you to the goal."

The Greek sages taught their disciples the wisdom "Know thyself", and this was no mere exhortation to explore the soul, or that aspect of soul which we call mind. They were pointing man to the spiritual Self, to know which in the intimacy of union is his goal as man. Ruysbroeck, one of the greatest religious mystics (1293–1381) said:

"Knowledge of ourselves teaches us whence we came, where we are, and whither we are going. We come from God and we are in exile; and it is because our potency of affection tends towards God that we are aware of this state of exile."

All the great religious teachers speak in their own language of self-naughting, self-denial, or detachment from the transient, and what underlies this teaching can be understood when we distinguish between, on the one hand, the self or individual soul plus its personality, and on the other hand the spiritual Self. William Law once said, "What could begin to deny self if there was not something in man different from self?" Jesus said, "If any man will come after me, let him deny himself, and take up his cross, and follow me. For whosoever would save his soul shall lose it: and whosoever shall lose his soul for my sake, shall find it." This was not an invitation to asceticism, or denying one's self *things*. It was pointing man to the mystic's goal. When we read the words, "Seek ye first the Kingdom of God and His righteousness and all these things shall be added unto you", they are commonly regarded as a piece of moral exhortation in regard to priorities. But if wherever we read the phrase "Kingdom of God" we interpret this as the spiritual Self (which God rules and sustains), we are probably much closer to the heart of His teaching.

✗ When the ego or self is truly denied, it is not destroyed but surrendered. It becomes the willing vehicle through which the Self or Spirit may find its expression. Thus Self-realisation is the complement of self-negation. It leads to such statements as Boehme's, "Not I, the I that I am, knows these things, but God knows them in me."

The same insight is expressed by Redwood-Anderson:[1]

"Say no more, 'Beethoven wrote the Ninth Symphony', for in so saying the weight is wrongly placed; say, rather, 'The Ninth Symphony has been written' . . . then, in parenthesis, 'by Beethoven'. For here the all-important point *that the Ninth Symphony has been written* receives its just emphasis, since it is only by the writing of the Ninth Symphony that Beethoven, as its writer, *is* Beethoven."

Nowhere is this insight expressed more frequently than in the Gita, where eloquent paradox abounds:[2]

". . . that which is without beginning, the Eternal Spirit which dwells in Me, neither with form, nor yet without it.

"Everywhere are Its hands and Its feet, everywhere It has eyes that see, heads that think, and mouths that speak; everywhere It listens; It dwells in all the worlds; It envelops them all.

"In all beings undivided, yet living in division, It is the upholder of all, Creator and Destroyer alike.

"It is the Light of lights beyond the reach of darkness; the Wisdom, the only thing that is worth knowing or that wisdom can teach; the Presence in the hearts of all."

Those who experience a moment of this basic Illumination frequently interpret it, with all its ecstasy, its fullness of love, and its wonder of inclusiveness, as an experience of God. There is of course a sense in which they are right. It *is* God immanent, but only so far as He is expressed through and in the Spirit of the Group-soul to which they belong. This experience is represented symbolically by (1) in the diagram.

In one of the scripts inspired by Myers[3] there is a remarkable essay on prayer, from which I quote:

"There are many degrees of union, many states which may be penetrated thus when we are in solitude and encompassed by a soundless calm. We first meet within the silence the gentle light of our own spirit. We are

[1] From an unpublished manuscript, *The Third World*
[2] Sri Purohit Swami, *The Geeta*, XIII, 13, 14, 17, 18 (Faber & Faber Ltd., 1935)
[3] Geraldine Cummins, *Beyond Human Personality*, pp. 135–6 (Psychic Press Ltd.)

stimulated by its rays. We are not yet in contact with the 'not-self', for this is the first state in meditation. When we enter the second state our consciousness becomes aware of the soul of the world. Thirdly and lastly, after much labour and much searching, we may within the stillness 'hear God' . . . You may not travel far, but you may—at least if you are fitted—in a few rare moments experience the divine state which those discarnate beings who are near the end of their journey realise supremely in the greater awareness that cannot be imaged in words, that passes all human understanding."

Perhaps (2) and (3) of the diagram may serve to symbolise these two higher states to which Myers refers in this passage. I should prefer, however, to replace Myers' expression "not-self" by the phrase "still higher Being to which the Spirit of the Group-soul is linked". I shall use the expression "contact with the not-self" in Chapters 4 and 5 to describe two lower forms of mystical experience than those which Myers had in mind. They are marked (1a) and 1b) on the diagram. The first of these is sometimes called Nature-mysticism, and this I take to be, in its fullest form, union with the Spirit or spirits behind Nature.[1] In lesser forms of Nature-mysticism the observer and the observed still retain their separateness even though all is "apparelled in celestial light". The experience is then strictly speaking psychical rather than mystical. In terms of the diagram I should say that the traverse (1a) is made prior to union of soul and Spirit. The second type of mystical experience (1b) is union with the not-self in the form of another self. This may appear paradoxical, but it is a valid distinction provided we recognise that within the Group-soul distinctions may exist without separateness.

If the reader will look again at the diagram, perhaps he will reflect upon the following thought. What is regarded as Being on one level may be regarded as Becoming from a higher one. Perfection on a lower level may be accounted imperfection from a higher. "Every truth," said Isaac Penington the Quaker, "is a shadow except the last. But every truth is substance in its own place, though it be but a shadow in another place. And the shadow is a true shadow, as the substance is a true substance."

---

[1] This may seem a reversion to animism. My view is that, rightly understood, animism is not far from the truth. If instead of "spirit" we read "sub-imaginal", the philosophy of Imaginism becomes relevant to mysticism.

Chapter

3

BASIC MYSTICAL EXPERIENCE

Thy light alone, like mists o'er mountains driven,
  Or music by the night wind sent
  Through strings of some still instrument,
  Or moonlight on a midnight stream,
Gives grace and truth to life's unquiet dream.

Love, Hope, and Self-esteem, like clouds, depart
  And come, for some uncertain moments lent.
  Man were immortal and omnipotent,
Didst thou, unknown and awful as thou art,
Keep with thy glorious train firm state within his heart.

SHELLEY

WHILE souls are clearly individualised, the associated Spirit is not in this sense individualised at all. We may think of the Spirit as the light which irradiates and the life which nourishes each of a group of souls, while not normally being intimately united with them. The disciplines and devotional practices undertaken by contemplatives in both East and West are attempts to lift the soul into that state in which the Spirit may stoop down to meet it. Some of these methods are described in Chapter 10. In this book we are confining our attention to ordinary people engaged in the world's work, to whom there have occurred rare moments when such an experience has been granted, by the grace of the Spirit. When the Spirit thus stoops down, it brings with it Bliss, Love and Wisdom so far beyond ordinary experience that the soul, trying afterwards to describe this, finds that the only adequate term is "God".

But as a traveller moving towards the coast—though still far inland—may observe the first seagulls and sense a new freshness in the air, so the presence of the Spirit is sometimes disclosed by signs and hints to those who can draw no nearer to its mystery. I shall begin by presenting a few accounts of this kind. Matthew Arnold would have called them

Murmurs and scents of the infinite Sea

Case 1 (G. A. F.)

"I was reading Proceedings of the 1950 Congress on Radiesthesia and Radionics—Eeman's article on circuit healing. Near the end of the article

38

there was reference to a passage by van Helmont on healing, written over 300 years ago. I became filled with a deep sense of awe (primarily) and wonder (secondarily). The feeling of exaltation persisted at least a quarter of an hour during the tram ride. Never in my life before had I so spontaneously wanted to *worship*. *Worship* had never been so real to me as an attitude of spirit. Why this passage should have given rise to this experience I cannot understand, especially as a friend of mine well-versed in psychical matters (and with some medical knowledge) was almost repelled by the article on account of what seemed to him to be dangers in the practice."

Case 2 (X. Y.)

"In 1903 our father took a stone cottage on the edge of a gorsey common for holidays and week-ends. Behind it was a wood which fell away to a brook in the bottom. It was the borderland between Wales and England. One day it came home to me that I was living on the borderland of two other countries—this world and the realm of spirit. It was like this.

"I was a child of eight or nine playing by myself. Perhaps my brothers and their playmates had been teasing me. They often did, because it made me storm and rage. I don't remember about that—but I do remember that I was alone, when—Something . . . made me pause; Something . . . was happening . . . just out of sight; Something . . . was coming . . . nearer and nearer.

"I looked hard. I could see the leafy trees and the golden glow of the gorse around me, but I could not see *What* was also present.

"I listened hard, until I could almost hear the brook far below in the bottom. No call nor voice came from *What* was coming . . . coming nearer and nearer to me, till *It* was breathing all around me, till the breath was coming through me—like the air itself—like a *Living One*—only stronger and more satisfying than any grown-up could be—far, far more so.

"It was all so strange and unexpected. I'd never dreamed of anything like this that was happening. I don't know how long it lasted, before I was left alone with the trees and the gorse. Yet *It* would always be there, whether I was shown *It* or not.

"I stood still for a long time. Some words which I must have heard came to me: 'God is Spirit'. So that was what *Spirit* meant! It was a surprise to me. Now, somehow, I knew what the words meant—or a tiny bit of what they meant.

"Then I walked slowly across the open course and went in among the bracken and tall gorse-bushes, out of sight of children and cottages. I wanted to be alone for a while with the Presence which was here, and yet not to be seen. There was a big flat stone there. I did what I had never done before. I knelt down beside the stone facing the woodside. Silently the words said themselves over and over again in my mind: God is Spirit—

and I longed with all my being for that strange, joyous event to be repeated. I waited in silence—hoping—but it did not happen again, like that. That event was a birth, a unique event. One is born, and then afterwards one has to grow up.

"I got tired of waiting. I got up and did another thing I hadn't done before, at least in this way, and for this purpose. I picked moss and thyme and little cranesbill with their leaves, and laid them carefully among the lichen on the stone. (They never had flowers in the bleak little hill-side chapel. I had never been inside a church, and did not know they had an altar.) Every day, for a long time, I used to go to the stone with flowers, and kneel down in silence, facing the woodside, hoping it would come again. It didn't.

"How do I know that this event was more than a child's play and fancy? Well! it has influenced my life ever since. It influenced me immediately in three ways. The kneeling at the stone set up a habit. Those fits of fury with my brothers ceased. This experience led me to help a family of three dirty neglected children who lived near.

"In addition to these immediate (and lasting) results, there is something else that witnesses to the reality of the child's experience. What was shown me then enabled me later to recognise that the biological Evolutionists, the Behaviourists and the Humanists were moving in other orders which were deposits from the realm of Reality. Even Bergson's *L'Evolution Creàtrice* seemed the attempt of a man who knew the Real, to try to fit it into sub-Real categories."

Case 3 (from *Surprised by Joy*, pp. 22-3), by C. S. Lewis (Geoffrey Bles, 1955)

"The first is itself the memory of a memory. As I stood beside a flowering currant bush on a summer day there suddenly arose in me without warning, and as if from a depth not of years but of centuries, the memory of that earlier morning at the Old House when my brother had brought his toy garden into the nursery. It is difficult to find words strong enough for the sensation which came over me; Milton's 'enormous bliss' of Eden (giving the full, ancient meaning to enormous) comes somewhere near it. It was a sensation, of course, of desire; but of desire for what? Not, certainly, for a biscuit tin filled with moss, nor even (though that came into it) for my own past—and before I knew what I desired, the desire itself was gone, the whole glimpse withdrawn, the world turned commonplace again, or only stirred by a longing for the longing which had just ceased. It had taken only a moment of time; and in a certain sense everything else that had ever happened to me was insignificant in comparison.

"The second glimpse came through *Squirrel Nutkin*; through it only, though I loved all the Beatrix Potter books. But the rest of them were merely entertaining; it administered the shock, it was a trouble. It troubled me with what I can only describe as the idea of Autumn. It sounds fantastic to say that one can be enamoured of a season, but that is something like what happened; and, as before, the experience was one of intense desire. And one went back to the book, not to gratify the desire (that was impossible—how can one *possess* Autumn?) but to reawake it. And in this experience also there was the same surprise and the same sense of incalculable importance. It was something quite different from ordinary life and even from ordinary pleasure; something, as they would say now, 'in another dimension'.

"The third glimpse came through poetry. I had become fond of Longfellow's *Saga of King Olaf*: fond of it in a casual shallow way for its story and its vigorous rhythms. But then, and quite different from such pleasures, and like a voice from far more different regions, there came a moment when I idly turned the pages of the book and found the un-rhymed translation of *Tegnner's Drapa* and read

> I heard a voice that cried
> Balder the beautiful
> Is dead, is dead—

"I knew nothing about Balder; but instantly I was uplifted into huge regions of northern sky, I desired with almost sickening intensity something never to be described (except that it is cold, spacious, severe, pale, and remote) and then, as in the other examples, found myself at the very same moment already falling out of that desire and wishing I were back in it."

Mr. Lewis had the above experiences as a boy. He has drawn attention to the common element in all three experiences, namely "an unsatisfied desire which is itself more desirable than any other satisfaction". Some years later when reading *Phantastes, a faerie Romance*, by George MacDonald, a visitation of the same essential Joy came to him, but on this occasion it lit up not merely the subjective, but also the objective world. Here is his account.

Case 4 (loc. cit., p. 170)

"Thus, when the great moments came I did not break away from the woods and cottages that I read of, to seek some bodiless light shining beyond them, but gradually, with a swelling continuity (like the sun at mid-morning burning through a fog), I found the light shining on those woods and cottages, and then on my own past life, and on the quiet room where I sat and on my old teacher where he nodded above his little *Tacitus*. For I now perceived that while the air of the new region made all my erotic and magical perversions of Joy look like sordid trumpery, it had no such disenchanting power over the bread upon the table or the coals in the grate. That was the marvel. Up till now each visitation of Joy had left the common world momentarily a desert—'The first touch of the earth went nigh to kill'. Even when real clouds or trees had been the material of the vision, they had been so only by reminding me of another world, and I did not like the return to ours. But now I saw the bright shadow coming out of the book into the real world and resting there, transforming all common things and yet itself unchanged. Or, more accurately, I saw the common things drawn into the bright shadow."

Case 5 (S. T.)

"I was packing up a house for my son—he had gone to sea, and his wife and family had gone off to our home in Wales. The furniture van had left, the house was empty, and I, feeling a little forlorn, was wandering round the garden thinking of the happy jolly times we'd had while they were living there. I caught sight in a flower-bed of a bright coloured ball which suddenly made me cry, and all at once I seemed to be in a changed atmosphere. It was a little alarming at first. Everything looked the same but seemed charged with something more real—very hard to explain. It was as if suddenly, for a flash, I was seeing the significance of things— material things being just symbols—like seeing familiar objects in another plane of existence. This curious feeling lasted about ten minutes, and then I was back to normal—but in those few moments I had sensed great happiness, and a sureness of something that I felt was eternal life."

COMMENTARY ON CASES I TO 5

The first three cases have much in common. All present a sudden upwelling of intense emotion occasioned by the drawing near of something which could not be apprehended by any of the senses, but which was *known* by some deeper part of the observer to be profoundly significant. Nothing in the outer world was felt to be an adequate cause: the reading of a fragment of history, a child's playing on familiar territory, the memory of a toy garden, the idea of Autumn, the verse about Balder, were scarcely relevant to the nature or intensity of the emotional experience. A psychologist might suggest that these small things aroused through association a repressed experience which was "abreacted" with a sense of great emotional release. There are elements in 3 and 5 which might lend some support to this, and they were recognised as such by the percipients. C. S. Lewis remarked that the desire for his own past came into the experience, and S. T. brought back to her mind "the happy jolly times we'd had"—although these were scarcely repressed! There is no doubt that the sensitive person with happy memories of the past sometimes feels moments of great poignancy at the realisation that they have gone for ever. Many of the English poets have struck the deepest chords of feeling when they have touched this theme. But allowing for this, Lewis says of the moment, "in a certain sense everything else that had ever happened to me was insignificant in comparison." Again, he says, "It was something quite different from ordinary life . . . something, as they would now say, 'in another dimension'." S. T. said, "It was as if suddenly, for a flash, I was seeing the significance of things." These accounts of profoundly heightened perception are not characteristic merely of emotional catharsis where a burden has been lifted and there is a wholesome release from tension, nor are they just the product of sentiment, however deep. There is about them "essential Joy", not melancholy. These accounts show the profound impression made upon the percipient by something not clearly apprehended and not at all understood, but inspiring "awe and wonder". "Never in my life before had I so spontaneously wanted to worship" applies to both 1 and 2 equally. Cases 2 and 3 mention the acute longing and desire to re-experience the mystery which drew so near. X. Y. said, "I longed with all my being for that strange, joyous event to be repeated." Lewis writes of the unsatisfied desire as "itself more desirable than any other satisfaction". The percipients are struggling with the inadequacy of language to convey the significance it had for them. This is not characteristic of sub-conscious irruptions, but it is what we should anticipate in a near approach of the Spirit to the human soul.

While all these accounts refer to an exaltation of soul, 4 and 5 are distinguished from the first three in that the external world shared in the glory. S. T. said, "I was seeing the significance of things—material things being just symbols . . . I had sensed great happiness, and a sureness of something that I felt was eternal life." C. S. Lewis said, "I saw the common things drawn into the bright shadow." The near approach of the Spirit enables the soul to realise that nothing it has loved can ever be lost. That to which our senses make response is but a precipitate from an eternal level where time cannot corrode, where space does not separate, and where there is no disenchantment. A. E. was constantly referring to this transforming influence of the Spirit upon common things:[1]

[1] *Song and Its Fountains*, p. 117 (Macmillan & Co. Ltd., 1932)

"I sometimes think that the spirit is so with us here because the purpose of the highest is the conquest and transmutation of the lowest ... I remember the promise of the god to the Thrice-Great Hermes, if he followed the straight way, was not beauty in a heaven-world, but an illumination in this world. 'It will everywhere meet thee and everywhere be seen of thee plain and easy, when thou dost not expect or look for it. It will meet thee waking, sleeping, sailing, travelling, by night, by day, when thou speakest or keepest silence. For there is nothing that is not the image of God.'"

In terms of the diagram, Cases 4 and 5 represent a traverse towards an incomplete union with the not-self, but it is from a point below the centre.

Case 6 (from *Saints and Revolutionaries* by Olaf Stapledon)

"Sometimes, when I am more than usually awake, I do have a deeply moving experience. There is nothing mysterious, or in any way magical about it. It is just ordinary experience of the world and oneself, only much more lucid and comprehensive. I cannot but regard it as the rightful compass-needle of my whole life. It may happen unexpectedly in response to some particular and even insignificant event, which now suddenly opens up vistas of significance; or it may come when I try persistently to 'get the feel of' being a self in relation to other selves and the rest of the universe. In either case it brings an unusually precise and poignant awareness both of my present surroundings and of things remote in space and in time. It seems to be simply a very comprehensive act of attention, an attending to everything at once, or to the wholeness of everything at once. And in response to all that this act of attention reveals I feel a very special emotion which I can describe only as a tension of fervour and peace. The experience is one which, if I were less sceptical, I might easily regard as some sort of contact with 'God'. But being sceptical I refrain from this interpretation. There may be a sense in which the old religious language is true, but in our day it is far less true than misleading ...

"But what about this 'something discovered in the depths of one's own being'? This I interpret as a metaphorical way of saying that in persistent contemplation of myself I discover, beneath all the personal desires which make up the everyday 'I', another desire or will, so alien from the everyday 'I' as to seem indeed another being. It is a detached will for the good, not for my good nor even for mankind's good, but for the good of the universe, whatever that may turn out to involve. I recognise that this will *ought* to be the supreme determinant of my conduct, and in a feeble sort of way I strive to submit my normal self to it. I recognise also that in some sense this will is a potentiality of all minds. Inevitably the awakening of a mind must lead it to this desire, this will. Evidently, then, this will is a very important factor in the universe. But what its metaphysical status is, I do not pretend to know.

"To say all this is to suggest merely my own reaction to an experience which I cannot at all clearly grasp, let alone describe. All I can say of it is that it gives meaning to life, that it is the supreme consolation, the supreme inspiration, and yet also, strangely, a most urgent spur to action."

Case 7 (K. J. S.)

"As a child an experience of what I may call perhaps 'the wonder of the infinite' appeared to me, and this experience, occurring from time to time, has given me a sense of God and of the end of the world's evil. It has led me to philosophy and, in the light of it, I have found myself conceiving a theory of things which has enabled me, I believe, to understand some at least of the views of the philosophical mystics.

"The 'wonder of the infinite' came to me, I think, as a promise of liberation: the finite world of things seemed a kind of enslavement to which I was subject; and to understand the Infinite—if I could—became, as I grew up, a sort of necessity which I could not avoid. I tried to philosophise on this subject, and it became clear to me by degrees that the Infinite I was looking for could only be the God of the mystics—the Being that *wholly is* apart from all limitation; the Being therefore that removes the prison doors of life and in unity with which the mind obtains complete and final freedom. To attain this freedom is to lose one's finite self and with it to lose those egoistic desires which are the source of evil. This may perhaps be called 'an intellectual illumination'; but it is also one associated with emotion—the emotion of joy. Some, I believe, have had an experience resembling this, and have associated it with some wonder-work of music or even with the sight of a flower. But my first experience, as far as I can remember, was not aroused by anything I saw or heard, and came as if from nowhere."

Stapledon's interesting account has close affinities with Cases 4 and 5. It is interesting that he remarks that while the experience could occur spontaneously it could also come through a conscious effort "to get the feel of being a self in relation to other selves and the rest of the universe". This looks like a modification of Ramana Maharishi's technique which consists of the soul's persistently pressing the enquiry "Who am I?" In effect it yielded a traverse (below the centre) to a partial union with the not-self. It brought to Stapledon a significant relationship with "things remote in space and time" (the (1a) type of traverse), and also with other selves (the (1b) type of traverse). The greatly expanded awareness of which he speaks, leading to the sense of belonging to a great unity, is one of the most characteristic features of mystical experience.

The second part of Stapledon's account is clear testimony to the existence of the Spirit as distinct from the soul, and to the fact that, once awakened, the soul finds its highest good in seeking earnestly for union with the Spirit. In his phrase the latter is "a detached will for the good of the universe". His own limited experience—which did not achieve the first stage—was nevertheless described as "the supreme consolation, the supreme inspiration, and yet also, strangely, a most urgent spur to action". This last observation is shared with the great mystics, who, after Self-realisation, have not despised the physical world, but have made of common things and common service a sacrament, and "seen them drawn into the bright shadow".

The common world seen in the light of the Spirit is known for what it is—the outermost garment of divinity. This is in contrast with the feeling expressed by K. J. S. that "the finite world of things seemed a kind of enslavement to which I was subject". Sometimes the latter (world-denying) attitude is found in an early stage of the mystic way. In order to realise the higher the lower may be temporarily ignored or devalued. Once the higher level is reached, the lower need not and should not be devalued. It can now for the first time be fully valued. It is like the ascent of a difficult mountain. A climber pays no attention to the steps he leaves behind: his advance requires concentration on the step just ahead. Once he has reached a safe eminence he can look back and see the steps below as a necessary part of the plan of ascent, even though the view from the higher position outshines by far that from the lower.

In realising that the soul's service of the Spirit is perfect freedom, and that denial of the self-centred being will finally destroy the egoistic qualities of pride, greed, fear and hatred, K. J. S. is in line with all the great teachers. "Our heart is like a fountain," said Tagore, "so long as it is driven through the narrow channel of self it is full of fear and doubt and sorrow, for then it is dark and does not know its end. But when it comes out into the open, on the bosom of the All, then it glistens in the sunlight and sings in the joy of freedom." [1]

We have to face the fact that strife and self-esteem, selfishness and ambition are factors which have had a long and inevitable part

[1] Rabindranath Tagore, *Letters to a Friend*, p. 80 (George Allen & Unwin Ltd., 1928)

to play in that long dim road of descent (of which we know so little) by which the germs of human souls appropriated, each for themselves, a finite instrument of action and perception (i.e. a mind) from the unformed collective mind. The citadel of self had to be defined and strengthened as an instrument of the soul's evolution. But at a certain stage in each soul's journey it gains a glimpse of this truth: that its higher evolution can only be attained by abandoning the methods through which it has arisen to conscious individuality—self-assertion at the expense of others. It comes to know that its higher evolution must be by love and service and humility. Finally, it glimpses the surpassing wonder of the Spirit—the great Being of which the true "I" is an aspect—and from then onwards union with it is the supreme good. I do not believe that this union means un-differentiated unity, however blissful. I do not hold that the union of soul and Spirit involves the loss of the soul's identity, but rather that its individuality is now surrendered and wholly devoted to the purposes of a greater Being in which it finds perfect freedom and perfect joy. This union makes such a soul a mature, fully conscious participant in the high activity and purposes of that Being. Do not let us be misled by the ecstatic language of the participants: this union is itself only one stage along the infinite way to God.

We pass on to some accounts of "Illumination" which is the term used for the union of soul and Spirit.

Case 8 (M. N.)

"Born in the mountains of Lebanon, I have always loved the solitude of high peaks and deep gorges, and found peace in the company of fantastic rock formations. I do not recall the day, the month and the year in which the experience took place. But I do recall the spot and the hour of the day. It was late summer afternoon, cool, clear and peaceful. I sat on a solitary rock, in the shade of a high wall of cliffs. Before me sloped to a deep gorge a stretch of land spattered with rocks and trees. Immediately to the left of me rose, almost perpendicularly, the rugged Mt. Saneen—one of the highest and loveliest peaks of the Lebanon range. Now and then I could hear the twittering of a bird, the bleating of a ewe, or the bellowing of a cow.

"Drifting from one thing to another, my thoughts were finally caught in the net of such questions as to How? and When? and Why? and by Whom? all this came to be. Such questions had long been besieging me, although I was yet between 20 and 21 years of age. Oblivious of everything about me, I began to feel like one labouring in an endless labyrinth and seeking a way out. The search, however, did not seem to oppress me. On the contrary, I felt as if goaded on and on, and as if I were on the verge of breaking through.

"Now subsiding, now flaring up, that feeling did not leave me until I suddenly emerged out of the labyrinth into a world flooded in dazzling light. How long I laboured in that labyrinth I do not recall. How long the sensation of light stayed with me—that also is hard to confine in seconds. It seemed like a fleeting twinkle of an eye; and it also seemed like an eternity.

"So poignant, so deep, was that experience, that for the rest of the day, and for many days after, I lived and moved as one lifted on wings and given a glimpse of Paradise. Nothing about me seemed alien to me, or unworthy of my love. I was at peace with all things.

"Since then I have had no such experiences. Yet not infrequently, while writing, meditating, or simply drifting aimlessly, I have had a feeling of a Presence about me guiding my hand and mind, and helping me to turn smoothly and safely what appeared to me to be dangerous curves in my spiritual literary and even social life."

Case 9 (Miss V. H.)

"This spiritual experience has haunted my life ever since April 1932. My life at that time was almost equally balanced between the carrying of well-nigh impossible burdens of responsibility, single-handed, in the family business after my father's death, and the spending of every available free moment at my church in service and bible-study and prayer. It was not an inward-looking community, and all its young people were encouraged to go out into the East End missions and clubs, and to serve in many ways. After an exhausting day, but with nothing in it to set it apart from many others, I had thrown myself down on to my bed at night, tired out. I seemed immediately to be gathered up into such a Light of Glory (and I mean visible and vibrant Light) of which I was part, that instinctively I fell on my knees at the bedside. How long I remained there I do not know. I slept soundly afterwards. The effects of the experience remained with me, in enhanced awareness of every form of life and experience, for at least three months, during which time I possessed boundless energy and vitality. It was, for me, an entrance into the Kingdom of Heaven, and every word as spoken in the Gospels by Jesus rang true to the facts of that experience. Eternal life was seen as a quality of life, which could be received and entered into here and now. Writings during that period were strangely prophetic; I awoke one night and wrote down seven short stanzas, one after the other, which came as I wrote them down. Examined rationally they are full of symbolism and unconscious liberation of pent-up emotions and experiences. I came to understand from within the experience of Paul, particularly when I tried to express something of my own awareness, and realised that I was open to serious question as to my mental stability, as Paul had been. But *I know that it happened*, and that is why I have remained in the service of the Church ever since. I could do no other, and I have sought no personal or private life."

Case 10 (C. A. M.)

"I will try to describe the experience as best I may, knowing that anything I can say will be quite inadequate. Many years before we were married, while I was an engineering student, we went for a walk into the hills. It was during this time that my companion manifested the symptoms of asthma. She has since said that she suffered during times of physical exertion, and during this expedition the symptoms were painful and extremely worrying to me. I had a feeling of despair and wondered what I would do. Even in those early days I was much attached to her, and to have to stand by and see her afflicted in this way drove me to desperation. We struggled on up the hill, and the next thing I noted was that the whole locality was illumined by an extraordinary, bright light. It was a cloudy and dull day and this extremely intense illumination did not appear to originate in any fixed centre, but was diffused equally throughout the entire terrain. Accompanying the light was the sense of the presence of an irresistible power wholly and utterly benevolent, and as far as I was concerned a feeling of complete happiness and well-being quite impossible to describe. The certainty of all-pervading and immutable love was so tremendous that I simply went on up the hill completely absorbed in this extraordinary experience and quite oblivious of the material surroundings. After an appreciable interval—I think a few minutes—the light gradually faded and I said to my companion, 'Did you see that?'

"But she had noticed nothing unusual, and so the experience was obviously psychical and not physical. However, she turned to me and said, 'My asthma is all gone'—and this disease has never reappeared.

"I have thought over this experience many times since, and have often wished to recapture the wonderful feeling of intense joy and happiness which accompanied it. None of the pleasures of life, the ecstasy of the poet and musician, nor the creative joy of the mathematician, can come within a million miles of the supreme happiness of this mystic event. Perhaps the scriptural phrase, 'The peace of God which passeth all understanding' comes nearest to expressing what can hardly be stated in words. I have felt since somewhat like the character in H. G. Wells' story *The Door in the Wall*, always seeking for the ultimate happiness and truth, which always eludes . . . In my own case, I think an important contributing factor was the outstanding spiritual character of my wife. Ever since I have known her she has exhibited psychic qualities, and the very highest human character and integrity . . . Another factor (and I cannot assess the part played by this, which may be considerable) was my slight knowledge of the religion known as Christian Science. This teaching, as I understand it, is based on two main metaphysical contentions. First, the distinction between appearance and reality, the sense data of the material world being considered as unreal and indicative of a real universe which lies behind it. Second, the adoption of the complete idealist metaphysic, somewhat after the pattern of Berkeley but with essential differences which I will not go into. I think I was prepared at this time to believe in the existence of a world of reality lying behind the sensible world, and this attitude may have contributed to the experience.

"I am grateful for the university training I received in science and mathematics in my engineering course, for by this means the mind was trained to an objective, factual approach to all problems. This seems to me the chief philosophical value of physics. In common with many persons so trained, the ultimate truth is the only value I seek after; anything else seems waste of time."

Case 11 (Mrs. M. E. A.)

"I have given much thought to trying to express my very precious one and only mystical experience. What would I not give for another?

"I was in bed at the time it happened, and my elder son, then aged 16, was very ill with congestion of the liver. I lay there for some time worrying about him, and then realised that no good could come of that state of mind; so I deliberately set to work to relax and reverse each fear-thought. Finally, I was meditating on God using the words, 'Be still, and know that I am God', and lingering mentally on what was implied by these wonderful words. Suddenly I became aware of a super-real state of being, with a completely relaxed feeling of blissful peace and trust in a Power of supreme beneficence and perfect harmony. One felt at one with it all and yet retained one's individuality. (This is one of the times when language fails, for it is a paradox when expressed in words, but while being experienced no difficulty exists.) The state also includes a feeling of coming home after weary wanderings, being surrounded by the welcoming warmth of loved and loving ones—only of course greatly intensified. There are no words to describe adequately what was the most intensely real and convincing spiritual experience of my life. I have no idea how long it lasted, but its significance for me has been incalculable and has helped me through sorrows and stresses which, I feel, would have caused shipwreck in my life without the clearly remembered refreshment and undying certainty of this one experience."

Case 12 (Miss I. W.)

" As I preamble, I think it necessary to say that at the time of this experience I was a non-church-goer, and still am; therefore I am not what is generally known as a religious person. The experience is far beyond my command of words and loses so much in the telling.

"During a period of dreadful alone-ness I became ill. For weeks my body dallied with death, and though I did not anticipate a reward of eternal bliss which orthodox Christians believe they will inherit immediately they pass on, I wanted to die, and during short intervals of comparative consciousness, I begged my doctors to let me do so, but they stubbornly refused to grant the request.

"In the earliest stages of a long convalescence, when my body was too weak to lift its head from the pillow, the dark and empty inertia in which I lay was filled with light. It did not come in a sudden blaze, but so gently that I scarcely knew when it came. Barriers were down; my aloneness had gone; I was at one with every living creature and thing. I *knew* that, despite almost overwhelming evidence to the contrary, a trinity of Truth, Beauty and Justice was the basis of life, and that 'somehow good would be the final goal of ill'. In that beautiful Biblical phrase, I *knew* that 'underneath were the Everlasting Arms'.

"The light—'illumination' is a better word—went as gently as it came, and left me with a legacy of knowledge that is beyond the bounds of belief and faith. Though my subsequent life has not justified retention of the knowledge, it has not been withdrawn, and never will be, because, being eternal, it is linked with the eternal in me."

Case 13 (L.)

This case is interesting because there was astral projection, preceding the mystical experience.

"The following spiritual experience occurred on November 26th 1927, when I was 27 years old. It seems impossible to explain this experience in words. While convalescing from a long and painful stomach ailment, I was preparing to retire, when suddenly I became very weak. Having been on a very light diet for many months, this weakness was understandable. But it seemed to me as though I might not be able to make it through another day, and I really didn't care whether I did or not. I was willing to place my hand in the Father's, knowing that He would care for me whatever happened. I was not in any pain. Slowly but surely, I managed to get into bed.

"Sometime during the night I was awakened by hearing my name called three times. Although I didn't recognise the voice, I thought at first it must be some member of my family, but could see no one and had heard no footsteps. This frightened me and I tried to call out but could make no sound! Nor could I move! This frightened me even more. Then a wave—an odd word to use, but I don't know how to explain it—started at my feet and moved rapidly upwards with peculiar pulling sensations at different parts of my body. As this wave reached my lungs, I struggled for breath, but to no avail. The breath and my consciousness went out of the body at the top of the head. My thought was that I was dying and this was the process of death.

"Throughout this entire experience I was always aware of being conscious, but after leaving the physical body I was no longer conscious of the personality, nor of being in any kind of a body. At first 'I', meaning consciousness, seemed to pass through darkness and was conscious of others being with me but did not see anyone or hear anything. After leaving the physical body I was never aware of anything connected with the five senses. That is why it is so difficult to explain in human terms. Time and space did not exist. After passing through the 'darkness', I emerged alone into radiant *white light, the Light of the Spirit*. You do not see this Light, you only know that you are immersed in it. Everything impressed on my consciousness while in the Light was by knowing, not by words. There was no process of thinking on my part. Somehow, the consciousness just knew. I was aware of Love—Universal Love—Peace, Joy, Bliss, Ecstasy—all we think of on the earthly plane of consciousness as being intangible—to such an extent that it is impossible to express it in words. I was aware of all Life as One and that Life is eternal. Also 'Service' seemed to be impressed upon me.

"Since there was no sense of time, I do not know how long I remained in the Light. Again, the period of darkness, and the knowing that others were with me through the darkness—then knowing that I must return to the physical body and it seemed then like a prison! This I did not want to do and prayed for release. All at once, after a slight shock, I realised my consciousness was again in my physical body and I was trying to establish breathing. This gasping for breath going out and coming back was the only unpleasant thing about the experience. Shortly after the breathing was established, the arms and legs and other parts of the physical body could be moved normally. My first thought was to give a prayer of thanks to God for such a marvellous experience. This I did and then went to sleep. The next morning I felt fine. For months after this experience I seemed to walk on air, but gradually, as time went on, there was a distinct lowering of consciousness. It could not be otherwise, I suppose, as the physical body lives in a physical world.

"It was afterwards that I had to put the experience into thoughts and then words in order to convey it to others. Naturally, I am convinced that the state of consciousness beyond mind, beyond personality, is *Reality, the Perfect State of Consciousness,* and that the *Light* my consciousness was immersed in during that experience is the Light spoken of in the Bible, the Light that lighteneth every man that cometh into the world.

"I have never had this experience again—or if I have, do not remember it consciously. I shall always be deeply grateful for it."

Case 14 (from *This Wondrous Way of Life* by Brother Mandus)

"I remember now (and I am always recalling it) the greatest experience in my life, that vital moment when I was baptised by the Holy Spirit within. For one perfect second, unexpected, unheralded, and while I was doing a trivial task, my personal mind and body were fused in *Light*: a breathless unbearable *Light-Perfection*, as intense as the explosion of a flash of lightning within me . . . In this timeless second I knew a Love, Knowledge and Ecstasy transcending anything I could understand or describe. I was lifted into the midst of God, in whom all people, all worlds, and every created life or thing moved and had their being. Perfection! Had I been suffering from the worst mental or physical disease known to man, in that *Light* I should instantly have been made *Whole*.

"In that moment I knew my Lord dwells within my own being, and within everyone else. In that one moment I knew the truth of His eternal reality, and that He is *All*, that my Father and I are *One*, that all people and the Father are *One*, and that we are all *One* with each other in spirit."

Case 15 (from *Recorded Illuminates* by Winslow Hall, M.D.)

B. E. B. is a middle-class English-woman of literary interests and occupation.

"I was 35 at the time of the experience. It happened thus: on April 13th 1905 at eight a.m. I was standing among pine trees looking out at the sky when suddenly the heavens opened, as it were, and caught me up. I was swept up and out of myself altogether into a flood of White Glory. I had no sense of time or place. The ecstasy was terrific while it lasted. It could have lasted only a minute or two. It went as suddenly as it came. I found myself bathed with tears, but they were tears of joy. I felt *One* with everything and everybody; and somehow I *knew* that what I had experienced was Reality and that Reality is Perfection.

"I would like to add that no words seem to me able to convey a thousandth part of the depth and reality of that experience, even so far as my own taste of it has gone. I fancy all one's normal faculties are first fused and then transcended. Immediately after this illuminative experience I jotted down the following rough verses . . .

"What I chiefly remember is the Light and the ecstasy of Perfection being Real. But what the verses chiefly connote is the sense of One-ness: which looks as though, at the time, it was this which had chiefly impressed me."

CHARACTERISTICS OF ILLUMINATION

It would have been possible to present many more accounts of Illumination, but we shall take these eight examples and see what conclusions can be drawn. The records of these experiences are from persons in very varied situations: a young man puzzling over the problems of existence in the mountains of Lebanon, an overburdened young woman working in London, an engineering student concerned about his friend's asthma, an anxious mother who decided to meditate upon God; two were women feeling alone and very weak in the early stages of convalescence from illness, and one was a young woman of literary inclinations among pine-woods. "The wind bloweth where it listeth, and thou canst not tell whence it cometh or whither it goeth. So is every one that is born of the Spirit."

If, as one may suppose, it is the quality of the soul which determines, in part, the possibility of union with the Spirit, one would not expect an attempt at assessment of *personality* to offer reliable guidance in generalising about conditions under which Illumination may come. How little can we know of anyone from an outward judgment! When we look at the accounts themselves, there is a remarkable measure of agreement.

(1) *The Appearance of Light.* This observation is uniformly made, and may be regarded as a criterion of the contact of soul and Spirit. The expressions used are very similar. "I suddenly emerged . . . into a world flooded in dazzling light." "I seemed immediately to be gathered up into (such) a light of Glory—and I mean visible and vibrant light, of which I was part." "This extremely intense illumination . . . diffused equally throughout the entire terrain." "Radiant White Light, the Light of the Spirit . . . you know you are immersed in it." "Mind and body were fused in Light—a breathless unbearable Light-Perfection." Frequently the appearance of the Light is sudden and dramatic, at other times it is gradual and gentle (Case 12). The comment of L. (Case 13) is particularly interesting. "I am convinced that the Light my consciousness was immersed in during that experience is the Light spoken of in the Bible, the Light that lighteth every man that cometh into the world."

(2) *Ecstasy, Love, Bliss.* Directly or by implication, almost all the accounts refer to the supreme emotional tones of the experience. "For many days after, I lived and moved as one lifted on wings and given a glimpse of Paradise" (Case 8). "It was, for me, an entrance into the Kingdom of Heaven" (Case 9). ". . . a feeling of complete happiness and well-being quite impossible to describe. The certainty of all-pervading and immutable love . . ." (Case 10). "Blissful peace and trust in a Power of supreme beneficence and perfect harmony . . . a feeling of coming home after weary wanderings . . ." (Case 11). "I *knew* that 'underneath were the Everlasting Arms' " (Case 12). "I was aware of Love—Universal Love—Peace, Joy, Bliss, Ecstasy . . . to such an extent that it is impossible to express it in

words" (Case 13). "In this timeless second I knew a Love, Knowledge and Ecstasy transcending anything I could understand or describe" (Case 14). "The ecstasy was terrific while it lasted" (Case 15).

(3) *The Approach to One-ness.* In the union of soul with Spirit, the former acquires a sense of unity with all things. Thus Mrs. M. E. A. of Case 11 said, "One felt one with it all and yet retained one's individuality. This is one of the times when language fails, for it is a paradox when expressed in words, but while being experienced no difficulty exists." It is doubtful if union with the Spirit can be realised without there following also a sense of union with the not-self. We are in a region of seeming paradox. I believe we must retain individuality without separateness for souls within a Group, and individuality without separateness for the Spirit in its relation to higher Beings. Here are some of the phrases used: "Barriers were down; my alone-ness had gone; I was at one with every living creature and thing" (Case 12). "I was aware of all Life as One and that Life is eternal" (Case 13). "In that moment I knew my Lord dwells within my own being, and within everyone else . . . and that He is *All*, that my Father and I are *One*, that all people and the Father are *One*, and that we are all *One* with each other in spirit" (Case 14). "I felt *One* with everything and everybody" (Case 15). Where, as in Case 8, the percipient does not mention it directly, the afterglow implies it, for the percipient says, "Nothing about me seemed alien to me, or unworthy of my love."

In Chapter 4 we shall find that union with the not-self (as Nature) appears to be possible without union with the Self or Spirit, but the approach to the latter union often leads to one of the traverses (1a) or (1b) of the diagram on p. 28.

(4) *Insights Given.* With the enormous vistas of the Spirit open to the soul for a moment of time, it is scarcely to be anticipated that the glimpses of knowledge brought back by different participants will be the same. All that we should ask of them is that they are not inconsistent with each other. A few of the more striking insights are these:

"Eternal life was seen as a quality of life, which could be received and entered into here and now" (Case 9).

"A trinity of Truth, Beauty and Justice was the basis of life, and that 'somehow good would be the final goal of ill' " (Case 12).

" 'Service' seemed to be impressed upon me" (Case 13).

"I am convinced that the state of consciousness beyond mind,

beyond personality, is *Reality, the Perfect State of Consciousness*"
(Case 13).

"Somehow I *knew* that what I had experienced was Reality, and
that Reality is Perfection" (Case 15).

(5) *Effect on Health and Vitality.* It is not surprising that several
of the participants refer to increased vitality. In some cases the
change is dramatic. Miss V. H. said, "For at least three months . . . I
possessed boundless energy and vitality." L. of Case 13, who had
been very weak and convalescent, said, "The next morning I felt
fine. For months after this experience I seemed to walk on air."
So intimate is the relationship of mind and body that any ecstatic
emotional experience (such as being "in love") is likely to have
stimulating effects on health. The instantaneous healing of asthma
in Case 10 is particularly interesting as occurring to the companion
of the participant who had not consciously entered into the mystical
experience. In Case 11 the mother's concern for her son did not
apparently have this result. It seems likely that the degree of rapport
of the two minds at the time may be a determining factor, but our
ignorance of the conditions of healing on all levels is still abysmal.
Brother Mandus' conviction is interesting: "Had I been suffering
from the worst mental or physical disease known to man, in that
Light I should instantly have been made *Whole.*" Tyrrell once said,
"There is no sense in which reality inheres in anything finite, except
in so far as it is an aspect of something which lies a step nearer to
the absolutely Real." As one who shares this view, I should expect
healing of the lower levels of the self to be quite possible—even
probable—in mystical experience.

(6) *Sense of Time obscured.* It is perhaps not of great importance,
but interesting to note that most of the participants had no clear
sense of the time involved. "It seemed like the twinkle of an eye:
it also seemed like eternity." "How long I remained there, I do not
know" etc. Intense mental concentration and strong emotions both
affect our sense of time's passage, as we know well in ordinary life.

(7) *Effects on Living.* Mrs. L., whose experience as a girl of 14
was related in Chapter 1, has written to me as follows:

"One doesn't have much experience of life at 14. Yet it was gloriously
satisfying. Even though I seemed to know all that ever was, and is, and
will be, I did not feel gorged with knowledge because my understanding
'remembered' only as much as could be illuminating to me at that time.
But that wasn't all I kept—and this is where a spark from the theory of
Imaginism flared into reality for me. I believe the rest has been **stored**,

because as I have grown out of each shell of understanding, some further part of that experience has been ready to illuminate the next phase of understanding. It is as though, at certain moments, one's soul says: 'There! Now you can see how that is part of the Eternal Truth', and the humdrum suddenly springs to life because one recognises its place in the Infinite. Even so, it is still cause for wonder to me that each further awakening comes in a flash.

"Perhaps it is this knowing without yet quite understanding which gives the living quality to such experiences. It lives because it is never completely understood and yet gives the promise of complete understanding in the future. Since from 14 to 40 is a period when so many changes and so much growth in understanding can take place, I cannot but notice and acknowledge this livingness. And I wonder could it be that this livingness is an essential quality of mysticism? Is it this that makes it so unforgettable for all who experience it?"

To the empiricist the fruits of mystical experience are necessarily most important testimony. Mrs. M. E. A. (Case 11) refers to "the most intensely real and convincing spiritual experience of my life" and continues, "Its significance for me has been incalculable and has helped me through sorrows and stresses which, I feel, would have caused shipwreck in my life without the clearly remembered refreshment and undying certainty of this one experience." This is necessarily subjective testimony, but it cannot lightly be set aside. Another says, "I have felt since the experience somewhat like the character in H. G. Wells' story *The Door in the Wall*, always seeking for the ultimate happiness and truth, which always eludes."

It is impressive to find that Arthur Koestler said,[1] as the immediacy of his experience ebbed away,

"I noticed some slight mental discomfort nagging at the back of my mind . . . Then I remembered the nature of that irrelevant annoyance: I was of course in prison and might be shot. But this was immediately answered by a feeling whose verbal translation would be: 'So what? Is that all? Have you got nothing more serious to worry about?' "

Along side of this may be placed the account given by B. E. B. of Case 15, of a lesser experience which she had twenty years later at the age of fifty-five. The occasion of this was an accident: she fell down a flight of eleven steps.

"Though the time occupied in it seemed quite long, my attention was instantly occupied by what seemed a point of bright light, within me, yet beyond me. It was like a diamond or a star, very bright and very

[1] See Chap. 4, Case 21

57

peaceful, very secure. My feeling was as though the point of white light addressed me saying: 'Don't be frightened even if your body is completely broken. I am safe, and I am all that matters'. I do not mean that there were any words, but this was the sense. I felt also that the white star was somehow the real meaning part of me.

"The effect of this experience was one of immediate calm. Though my body was falling, and I knew it, all fear and bewilderment had ceased. At the end of the fall I found myself on the stones outside my door, shaken, and with a broken wrist, but quite undismayed, and indeed triumphant. I was living a long way from a doctor; but though I had a telephone, it never occurred to me to seek help, so thoroughly happy did I feel because of that sight of the shining spark. I had not the sense of unity which was so strong in my first experience, but I recognised that this was the very same kind of light as that which overwhelmed me then— though only a spark and inside me, yet beyond the body, instead of being everywhere and with no sense of 'me' at all. It brought me the same infinite reassurance, and again it has lasted. It showed me once more, beyond all 'reasoning', that we have Life within, compared with which the life of the body is but a shadow, evanescent, and indeed of no value compared with the other.

"The wrist, which was never 'set', except by Nature, is now a bit crooked and a little weak . . . yet I never see its slight deformity or feel its trifling incapacity without feeling with unspeakable gratitude, 'But what a tiny price to pay for such certitude'."

It seems that sometimes the Spirit stoops down with tender solicitude for the soul—its exiled child in the midst of suffering. It was said of a famous figure of the ancient world that "he endured as seeing Him who is invisible". Happy are they who amid the changes and chances of this mortal life are granted this seeing and find this certainty.

Chapter

4

DISCLOSURE OF THE NOT-SELF: (I) NATURE

> When hill, tree, cloud, those shadowy forms
> Ascending heaven are seen,
> Their mindless beauty I from far
> Admire, a gulf between;
>
> Yet in the untroubled river when
> Their true ideas I find,
> That river joined in trance with me,
> Becomes my second mind.
>
> SIR GEORGE ROSTREVOR HAMILTON [1]

IN the previous chapter I expressed the view that the primary and fundamental mystical experience is union of soul and Spirit—the individualised self with the transcendent Self. Following on this there is usually, if not inevitably, an awareness of an intimate relationship with the not-self, i.e. with the world of Nature and with other selves. We noticed that this "traverse" could be made before the primary experience was complete.

Nature-mysticism, as it is called, ranged from the sense of a new glory and beauty in familiar things to a sense of complete one-ness with them. From some of the accounts given in this chapter it might seem that it exists *per se*. My own view is that it exists rather as a consequence of the drawing near of Spirit to soul, whether the latter consciously recognises this or not. I agree with Lawrence Hyde[2] when he said, "No man can perceive the not-self in its true aspect until he has discovered within his own being that Self for which it exists." I believe, however, that there are steps on the way to this discovery.

I propose first to present accounts of experience, making brief comment where there are special points of interest. Afterwards I shall consider the issues raised such as the relation of the mind to the external world, of the observing subject and the observed object.

Case 16 (Mrs. A. D.)

"One day when I was playing golf my companion lost a ball. As I searched for it I stopped beside a young wattle tree coming into blossom.

[1] From *The Carved Stone* (Heinemann Ltd., 1952)
[2] *The Nameless Faith*, p. 172 (Rider & Co. Ltd.,)

I stood and gazed at it quite delighted, taking in every detail, giving it my whole attention. Then a really indescribable thing happened. As I stared at it, its beauty grew until it was transformed to a living glowing pitch of *intense* beauty past all imagining. It remained so for at least thirty seconds, during which I was aware of my almost incredulous amazement. (Actually, I had the feeling that I could have gone on seeing it in its transformed state had I been able to sustain it, i.e. to maintain some sort of focus.)"

I do not regard this experience as mystical, but rather one of clairvoyant perception. It will be observed that the sense of selfhood is clearly preserved throughout.

Case 17 (L. H. M. B.)

"It was on a night in October about eleven p.m. I suddenly found myself out of the body floating over a Highland moor, in a body as light or lighter than air. There was a wood at the side of the moor and the clouds were drifting past the moon and a cool fresh wind was blowing. I found that I didn't mind the wind as I should have done had I been in my physical body, because I was *at one* with it. The life in the wind and the clouds and the trees was within me also, flowing into me and through me, and I offered no resistance to it. I was filled with glorious life. All the time, in the margin of my consciousness, I knew where my earthly body was, and that I could return to it instantly if danger threatened. The experience may have lasted a few minutes or a few seconds, I cannot tell—for I was outside time. I came back greatly invigorated and refreshed, and very much alive. I remember thinking that if this was what the so-called dead experienced, how much more vitally alive they are than we are here."

This is a self-confessed out-of-the-body experience which is introduced here because the account uses phrases which are characteristic of many descriptions of Nature-mysticism. It is important to distinguish the mystical level of experience fr.... that of astral projection[1] while recognising, of course, the possibility that mystical experience may be attained from the projected state just as it may from the normal incarnate state. The phrase "at one" obviously does not mean here a mergence of subject and object, but a harmonious co-existence of the observer in her astral body with the external world.

Case 18 (M. I. D.)

"It was one of those gloriously lovely days that one sometimes sees in early Summer in England—a cloudless vividly blue sky with brilliant

[1] Those who are unfamiliar with this phenomenon may consult Chap. 10 of *The Imprisoned Splendour* by R. C. Johnson.

sunshine. It was morning. The air was shimmering with the moisture from the evaporating dew. I was walking on the lawn looking at the masses of flowers in the herbaceous border. As a gardener I was interested in what was coming up into flower; as an artist I was enjoying the combination of colour, light and shade. Suddenly, as I paused in contemplation, I was 'lifted' into another world (plane or dimension?). I did not seem to be inside myself though I was still looking normally at the flower border. Everything had become a thousand times more brilliant. Everything had also become transparent. But what was so amazing was the fact that I was not only seeing the colours—I was hearing the colours! Every colour was an indescribably exquisite musical sound, the whole making a harmony that no instruments could produce. I do not know how long this illumination lasted, perhaps not more than a second or two, but as I came back to earth, so to speak, I knew that I had been in Reality.

"The memory of it has remained vivid and real ever since, and has brought me the greatest happiness and understanding. Now I *know*. I am truly thankful for this gift of knowledge."

I regard this case as comparable with 16 and probably one of clairvoyance. This phrase "I did not seem to be inside myself" suggests some measure of astral projection—or at least displacement. Under these conditions extra-sensory perception, as we call it, becomes normal astral perception. The most interesting feature was the synaesthesia. The "seeing" of sound and "hearing" of colour are phenomena reported by a number of communicators as observations of the astral level,[1] and they occur sometimes under the influence of LSD and mescalin.[2] If the brain is an organ of limitation, it is not surprising that apparently independent sensations on the physical level should be disclosed as related on higher levels of mind. A still higher apprehension would doubtless disclose the unity which precipitates itself into sensory variety on the lower levels. This kind of experience is a happy foretaste of the wonder and beauty of the world on its higher levels—of which we may some day hope to know more. But as long as subject and object, the observer and the observed are separate, we have not risen to the mystical level.

Case 19 (from *Art Digest*, February 1953, "A John Ferren Profile" by J. Fitzsimmons)

The author of this article on the American artist, John Ferren, describes a mystical experience which the latter had.

"It happened one summer afternoon while he was walking in the hills

---

[1] Anthony Borgia, *Life in the World Unseen*, p. 16 (Odhams Press Ltd.); Geraldine Cummins, *Travellers in Eternity*, p. 137 (Psychic Press Ltd.)

[2] R. H. Ward, *A Drug-Taker's Notes*, p. 84 (Victor Gollancz, 1957)

near Berkeley with his friend Kenneth Rexroth. On many previous occasions he had had 'a sudden sense of identity with certain places in Nature ... coupled with a sense of well-being ... a sense of identity with the spot in volume, an awareness of a dimension which encompassed the spot in minute detail, but which was certainly not of the customary three dimensions'. On this occasion, not only was the experience greatly intensified, it was accompanied by a sudden realisation of the common ground, or texture of all things. Here is how Ferren describes it:

" 'I asked my friend if he felt anything peculiar and he answered "No". I placed my hand on a tree-trunk. I instantaneously felt that every element of the landscape was alive, the light, air, ground and trees. All were inter-related, living the same life, and (this is important to my art) their forms were all interchangeable. The forms of things were only the particular expressions of an energy, or substance, which they all shared in common.'

"From that time on, Ferren ceased to be concerned with the appearance of things. He decided that as an artist his function 'was to reproduce in the spectator the sense of unity' which he had experienced so incontrovertibly. He goes on to say, 'I foresaw a directly evocative art ... For the artist to copy the self-evident beauties of nature was merely to praise. His true function was not praise of Nature but the establishment of an identity with Nature wherein he functioned with and like nature.' This is of course a very Chinese attitude, and Ferren says, 'Well, I think I am very Chinese in this respect'."

Case 20 (from *Corporal Tune*, Chap. 7, by L. A. G. Strong)

"The ledge was an enchanted place. Here one fine day this summer Ignatius had sat for seven hours, absorbed, watching the play of light on sea, and seven hours had passed as one. The wind altered every few minutes, the sun wheeled across from Ignatius's left shoulder to his right, the preoccupied sea changed its mind and wandered; then by degrees all accustomed images of thought left him, there were neither words nor metaphors, sea and earth and sky existed on their own terms, and he was gradually absorbed into all he saw, till he lost human consciousness, and became one of many objects, a part of the coast, drained of his identity, persisting mindless like a patch of obstinate sunlight gleaming on the water a mile from shore, a patch of which he was without thought aware, just as without thought he was aware of himself sitting on the ledge: dimly, from time to time aware, but without distinction between his body pressing upon the rock or the rock pressing up against his body: human consciousness passed out from him, yet not into sleep; into no blurring of sense: something clear and shining, wind touched, shadow crossed: something at once firm and rooted like the sun-warmed rock, cool and flowing like the water, outspread like the pine branches, high as the clouds, volatile as the air—something with perceptions extended in all these, something infinitesimal yet supreme, fragment and whole, wave, beam of light, path that the gull had not yet taken through the air: something which, when the elated mind tried to realise it, broke up thus into a thousand facets, but which in spells of deepest experience sank to a luminous sense of peace; light and water and stillness in a pool as wide as the sky. It was an experience not to be put into words, for the effort to find words at once split up the central unity of awareness into a series of particular visions; creating multiplicity; shattering a timeless exaltation into restlessness, breaking eternity into succession and the intervals between one object and another. Just as, when three parts asleep, one can at will remember the position of one's limbs, and then relax to a tide of dream, so Ignatius could in multiplicity remember himself and divide the place into units, or empty himself and be one with the scene of which he was a part. Life, or spirit, call it what one would, was manifested variously in living things and in trees and air and stones. Ignatius for a while had seen the barrier broken down, relapsing through his special identity to the principle which he expressed, which all this coast expressed, affirming his union with it and its union with him; regressing from the details imposed by time to a truth outside it.

"When he came to himself, his limbs stiff and numb, his mind was so charged with luminous wisdom and tranquillity that for a few moments he knew that there was no human problem he could not solve, and that, by the light that was slowly fading within his mind, he could illumine his own life and the lives of others. But the light faded; the great satisfying chord hummed away over the far horizon, and there remained only the faint piping notes of petty detail, the straying unresolved motifs and burdens of the symphony."

Case 21 (from *The Invisible Writing*, pp. 351-2, by Arthur Koestler)

The author describes how in a prison cell he had, with a piece of wire scratching on the wall, recovered Euclid's proof that the number of primes is infinite. He felt an aesthetic enchantment, and says:

"The significance of this swept over me like a wave. The wave had originated in an articulate verbal insight; but this evaporated at once, leaving in its wake only a wordless essence, a fragrance of eternity, a quiver of the arrow in the blue. I must have stood there some minutes, entranced, with a wordless awareness that 'this is perfect—perfect'; until I noticed some slight mental discomfort nagging at the back of my mind— some trivial circumstance that marred the perfection of the moment. Then I remembered the nature of that irrevelant annoyance: I was of course in prison and might be shot. But this was immediately answered by a feeling whose verbal translation would be: 'So what? Is that all? Have you got nothing more serious to worry about?'—an answer so spontaneous, fresh and amused as if the intruding annoyance had been the loss of a collar-stud. Then I was floating on my back in a river of peace, under bridges of silence. It came from nowhere and flowed nowhere. Then there was no river and no I. The I had ceased to exist.

". . . When I say 'the I had ceased to exist' I refer to a concrete experience that is verbally as incommunicable as the feeling aroused by a piano concerto, yet just as real—only much more real. In fact its primary mark is the sensation that this state is more real than any other one has experienced before—that for the first time the veil has fallen and one is in touch with 'real reality', the hidden order of things, the X-ray texture of the world, normally obscured by layers of irrelevancy.

"What distinguishes this type of experience from the emotional entrancements of music, landscapes or love is that the former has a definitely intellectual, or rather noumenal content. It is meaningful, though not in verbal terms. Verbal transcriptions that come nearest to it are: the unity and interlocking of everything that exists, an inter-dependence like that of gravitational fields or communicating vessels. The 'I' ceases to exist because it has, by a kind of mental osmosis, established communion with, and been dissolved in, the universal pool. It is this process of dissolution and limitless expansion which is sensed as the 'oceanic feeling', as the draining of all tension, the absolute catharsis, the peace that passeth all understanding . . . there remained a sustained and invigorating, serene and fear-dispelling after-effect that lasted for hours and days."

Koestler tells us that he never knew how long the experience itself lasted. He also says that while, in their beginning, such experiences occurred two or three times a week, the intervals afterwards lengthened to the order of a year. He says, "They filled me with a direct certainty that a higher order of reality existed, and that it alone invested existence with meaning."

Case 22 (F. W.)

"I prayed for help from out of the darkness, and there, behold, as a flash, the scene changed. All became alive, the trees, the houses, the very stones became animated with life, and all became vibrant with the life within them. All breathed effulgent light, vivid sparkling light, radiating out and in every direction; and not only that, but everything seemed to be connected with everything else. Although all separate forms, and all vibrating with their own intensity of life, yet they all seemed to be connected by their vibrations into one whole thing, as the different coloured parts of a picture are yet of the same picture, although when one is near to it each different object can be viewed separately.

"So in the same way with natural objects—by which I mean every common and ordinary thing of which we are conscious, including our bodies—they are but parts of one intensive radiant activity, every particle endowed with life and light of a quality that cannot be conceived of, for, although of the power of the arc lamp, there is no sense of glare or strain. And we are surrounded by this glorious world of light all the time!"

Case 23 (Mrs. M. S.)

"I suppose many people have had the experience I will try to describe. I have had it less than a dozen times in my life. It cannot be induced: it comes for no apparent reason. The first thing seems to be a feeling of floating or buoyancy, and one seems to be breathing a different sort of air. Although one's normal surroundings can still be seen one feels caught up in the air. (I can't describe it.) Everything, even the air, seems scintillating, vibrating with life. For example, it once came on me in the train going down Shap between Penrith and Fenholm. The lochs, hills and trees were all intensely *alive*. The colours were intensely bright and shining. I said to myself, 'Am I seeing the reality behind the physical aspect of Shap?' I don't know. Anyway, the great thing which is common to all these experiences is the feeling of perfect happiness, peace and joy that comes with them; also the knowledge that grief, loss and unhappiness aren't real. You are, for these few moments, somewhere where they *don't exist*. You know they do exist because you are probably suffering them at the time of the experience, but when you are in the experience they aren't there. It would not be possible to feel sorrow, then. I have always thought that 'the peace which passeth all understanding' was just that sensation. There is also consciousness of a white light. But I do not associate any spiritual personages with this sort of experience.

"There is another sort of feeling that comes when in *great* grief, after much prayer. This is another sort of feeling of 'peace' and brings with it the sense of spiritual presences, but it is possible that this may be also due to the fact that in great agony of loss there are times when one just *can't* feel any more through sheer nervous shock and exhaustion. It is entirely different from the white light experiences which, though impossible to describe, are a joy beyond words."

Case 24 (J. P. W.)

"Though I was undergoing pneumothorax and was experiencing the progression of rheumatoid spondylitis, I was not in great turmoil, for I had reached a point where it seemed to me that men were alonenesses together in this. I believed our condition was essentially meaningless . . .

"On this particular day I wandered alone out to a meadow-like area and sat down against a pine. The day was beautiful and warm: the time shortly before noon . . . I do not know how long I sat, but after a period of 'empty' enjoyment, I became intensely aware of many of the objects which were in the area. The rocks, the trees, the birds, the stream, the clouds, the flowers, became extremely meaningful to me. I realised the rocks, trees etc. were I; I they; all brothers. And I was exceedingly joyful in realising this kinship.

"From this awareness, we flowed into, became, the great Golden Light—the rocks, trees, etc. and this 'I' were no longer just kindred separatenesses. We disappeared. We became the Light which is Love, Bliss. This Light was neither hot nor cold; but Love, Consciousness, Eternity, It. No name was given, nothing was heard. Nor did this 'I' then or after experience frenzy or any sort of fitful or emotional upheaval. Rather Peace, Certainty was known.

"Because of the experience I know that *everything* involved in this process is God, is Love, Light, Bliss . . . that everything is in migration, movement, towards the Great Awakening to That which, in essence, everything is. Nothing, nothing is excluded from the 'redemptive' process. Not only all men, but men and rocks and stars and trees are brothers, are divine, and carry within them the splendour awakening to Itself.

"After this event I somehow knew that this was the last time [of incarnate existence], that there would be no more I[s] for this soul's development . . . that it 'had crossed the line into the land of no to-morrows'. Yet I also realised that we cannot really go Home until everything goes Home again."

Case 25 (H. M.)

"One evening at this time I was quietly playing over the Mendelssohn *Lieder ohne Worte* and turned to the *Duetto* which has always made an especial appeal to me . . . When I went to bed I fell asleep almost at once, but towards midnight awoke suddenly with an experience impossible to describe; I cannot find words to fit. At any rate after what was probably ten minutes or so I fell into a deep sleep. The next day I did not recall the experience or of having wakened, and it did not enter my mind again for a comparatively long time afterwards. But later I realised that from the day immediately following that experience I noticed a difference in everything around me.

"I noticed a difference in my fellow-man, in the animals, in the trees and flowers, and as days wore on I saw in every individual, even in the horses and the cats and the dogs, a wonderful glow of beauty, a serene whiteness absolutely pure. It was not the aura as we are told—it was greater than that. Faces shone with serenity and a glowing loveliness; even the so-called ugliest was a picture of perfect beauty. I looked everywhere and at everyone, so much so that I feared I should be rebuked. I even saw it in photographs; in pictures of native African and Chinese tribes—far from being objects of beauty according to our eyes and standards. To test myself I inspected everywhere and everything.

"Where, formerly, on every hand I had seen only the imperfections of my fellow-man, I saw now inherent nobility, purity, goodness and beauty, shining out and overshadowing the baser qualitities. Look where I would I could not escape it, and it grew in intensity. It reminded me of Francis Thompson's poem *The Hound of Heaven*.

"All my life I have been of a sceptical turn of mind, prone to measure by first impressions, which, generally speaking, have been confirmed, but it has always been easier for me to see the lower than the higher qualities—with exceptions, of course. On every hand now, however, I met with a constant radiation of kindness, thoughtfulness, generosity, glowing loveliness—and woman appeared more spiritual than man. I was simply overwhelmed as by a flood from all quarters. Where, formerly, it had been difficult to encounter certain associations with equanimity this difficulty was swept away and I looked for it in vain. What struck me very forcibly was that no change was apparent to me in the faces of those whom I held, and who held me, dear. You can imagine how intently I scanned the faces of my family on their return.

"The change was wrought to my eyes in the world apart from me. But it was so wrought that I saw there was no such thing as separateness—no such thing as the world apart from me—and the unity of all life, of all existence, was spread out before me, as though a vast curtain had been lifted and the full scene exposed to my gaze. Words fall lamentably short of true description.

"This faculty remained with me for several weeks, gradually decreasing in intensity from the particular time when a harsh word spoken by another to a third person, both of those persons being unknown to me, tore through me as though it were ripping to pieces my very being. That, I shall never forget. It was at that particular moment that I suddenly realised the meaning of 'vicarious atonement'. From that time on my sensitiveness became less acute, and its *particular* delicateness is *now* comparatively absent. But, I find that *at will* all the baser elements fade into nothingness, and only what (at the risk of being styled 'egoist') I might call the divinity of nature and of man is then visible to me.

"Since that time I have seen in certain music and poetry an inner mystical meaning, and to tell you the truth, I am saddened when I find that meaning seems to be quite unsensed so to say by others around me. You know how Walt Whitman seems at times to be involved and somewhat incomprehensible. Well, some of his poems, especially the *Song of the Open Road*, are as plain now as though written in words of one syllable for a child. The innermost meaning, that is to say. I can see also now with Wordsworth in his lines 'The world is too much with us . . .' They got into touch knowingly or unknowingly with that Inner Spirit, which was so evident to me during those many weeks, so that they naturally turned to a means of expression easiest to them. Their experience seems to have been so ineffable that poetry was the medium which lent itself as most adaptable to their thought—a medium to try to express a part-comprehension of infinity, if that were possible.

"As one gazes into a pool and sees the fish one takes no cognisance of the different varieties of fish, but connotes them only as fish. There is to one's mind complete unity of all such creatures, irrespective of individual differences, by reason of the fact that they all abide in the same element. Well! that is the nearest description I can give you of the manner in which all existence now appears to me. There is absolute unity in all creation, and one motive power. And, for another thing, I sensed with entire conviction that there *is* no time and there *is* no space.

"The curtain has now been rolled down and I am left desolate as it were. But, also, I am left with knowledge where I formerly possessed only speculation."

Case 26 (M. P. M. from *The Atlantic Monthly*, pp. 590-7, 1916)

The account was written about two years after the experience. The lady had undergone a surgical operation, following which there had been a short period of acute mental depression. She supposed it was physical in origin, but wondered at the time whether, under the anaesthetic, she had unearthed some dreadful secret—such as that there was no God. It was a cloudy and rather windy day in March and the convalescent patient had been wheeled out into a porch.

"I cannot now recall whether the revelation came suddenly or gradually; I only remember finding myself in the very midst of those wonderful moments, beholding life for the first time in all its young intoxication of loveliness, in its unspeakable joy, beauty and importance. I cannot say exactly what the mysterious change was. I saw no new thing, but I saw all the usual things in a miraculous new light—in what I believe is their true light. I saw for the first time how wildly beautiful and joyous, beyond any words of mine to describe, is the whole of life. Every human being moving across that porch, every sparrow that flew, every branch tossing in the wind, was caught in and was a part of the whole mad ecstasy of loveliness, of joy, of importance, of intoxication of life.

"It was not that for a few keyed-up moments I imagined all existence as beautiful, but that my inner vision was cleared to the truth, so that I *saw* the actual loveliness which is always there, but which we so rarely perceive; and I knew that every man, woman, bird and tree, every living thing before me, was extravagantly beautiful, and extravagantly important. And as I beheld, my heart melted out of me in a rapture of love and delight. A nurse was walking past; the wind caught a strand of her hair and blew it out in a momentary gleam of sunshine, and never in my life before had

I seen how beautiful beyond all belief is a woman's hair. Nor had I ever guessed how marvellous it is for a human being to walk. As for the internees in their white suits, I had never realised before the whiteness of white linen; but, much more than that, I had never so much as dreamed of the mad beauty of young manhood. A little sparrow chirped and flew to a nearby branch, and I honestly believe that only 'the morning stars singing together, and the sons of God shouting for joy' can in the least express the ecstasy of a bird's flight. I cannot express it but I have seen it.

"Once out of all the grey days of my life I have looked into the heart of reality; I have witnessed the truth; I have seen life as it really is— ravishingly, ecstatically, madly beautiful, and filled to overflowing with a wild joy and a value unspeakable. For those glorified moments I was in love with every living thing before me—the trees in the wind, the little birds flying, the nurses, the internees, the people who came and went. There was nothing that was alive that was not a miracle . . .

"Besides all the joy and beauty and that curious sense of importance, there was a wonderful feeling of rhythm as well, only it was somehow just beyond the grasp of my mind. I heard no music, yet there was an exquisite sense of time, as though all life went by to a vast unseen melody. Everything that moved wove out a little thread of rhythm in this tremendous whole. When a bird flew it did so because somewhere a note had been struck for it to fly on; or else its flying struck the note; or else again the great Will that is Melody willed that it should fly. When peopled walked, somewhere they beat out a bit of rhythm that was in harmony with the whole great theme.

"Then the extraordinary importance of everything! Every living creature was intensely alive and intensely beautiful, but it was as well of a marvellous value. Whether this value was in itself or a part of the whole I could not say: but it seemed as though before my very eyes I actually beheld the truth of Christ's saying that not even a sparrow falls to the ground without the knowledge of the Father in Heaven. Yet *what* the importance was, I did not grasp. If my heart could have seen just a little further I should have understood . . . I have a curious half-feeling that somewhere, deep inside myself, I know very well what this importance is, and always have known; but I cannot get it from the depth of myself into my mind, and thence into words. But whatever it is, the importance seemed to be nearer to beauty and joy than to an anxious morality. I had a feeling that it was in some way different from the importance I had usually attached to life. It was as though perhaps that great value in every living thing was not so much here and now in ourselves as somewhere else . . . Certainly that unspeakable importance had to do with our relationship to the great Whole; but what the relationship was, I could not tell. Was it a relationship of love towards us, or only the delight in creation? But it is hardly likely that a glimpse of a cold Creator could have filled me with such an extravagant joy, or so melted the heart within me. For those fleeting lovely moments, I did indeed and in truth love my neighbour as myself. Nay, more; of myself I was hardly conscious, while with my neighbour in every form, from wind-tossed branches and little sparrows flying, up to human beings, I was madly in love. Is it likely that I could have experienced such love if there were not some such emotion at the heart of Reality? If I did not actually see it, it was not that it was not there, but that I did not see quite far enough . . .

"And all the beauty is for ever there before us, for ever piping to us, and we are for ever failing to dance. We could not help but dance if we could see things as they really are. Then we should kiss both hands to Fate and fling our bodies, hearts, minds and souls into life with a glorious abandonment, an extravagant delighted loyalty, knowing that our wildest enthusiasms cannot more than brush the hem of the real beauty and joy and wonder that is always there . . .

"And though I have never again touched the fulness of that ecstatic vision, I know all created things to be of a beauty and value unspeakable, and I shall not fail to pay homage to all the loveliness with which existence overflows . . . Sometimes still, when the wind is blowing through trees or flowers, I have an eerie sense that I am almost in touch with it. The veil was very thin in my garden one day last summer. The wind was blowing there, and I knew that all that beauty and wild young ecstasy at the heart of life was rioting with it through the tossing larkspurs and rose-pink Canterbury bells, and bowing with the foxgloves; only I just could not see it. But it is there—it is always there—and some day I shall meet it again. The vision will clear, the inner eye will open, and again all that mad joy will be upon me."

The reader will, I think, be interested to know that a physician, Dr. Cabot, ascertained that no drugs, fever, fasting or other obvious factors could he held responsible for the experience. He drew a parallel between it and the viewing of a sunset with the unaccustomed half of the retina. "Ordinary perception", he said, "is untrue, because it has become blinded by over-use. It is calloused and numb. But when (by standing on our heads, or approaching that attitude in more comfortable ways) we suddenly see things afresh, the new truth is beautiful truth." Satiety is, he said, the normal state of most of us in adult life, and he concludes that ten days of hospital confinement followed by convalescence and renewed contact with the world "cracked the crust of habit".

If it were as simple as this we should all be booking ten days in hospital (or perhaps prison would be more effective). Moreover, we could wish that many modern writers would do some standing on their heads.

Commenting on this remarkable case: its lyrical description and the very skilful use of words almost obscure from us the fact that M. P. M. did not quite attain to union of soul and Spirit. She herself recognised that this culmination required her to go a little farther. "I did not not see quite far enough," she said. Lover and a beloved world are there in an ecstasy of enjoyment, but for all its overflowing wonder the experience just falls short of union. She refers, however, to many insights gathered from the experience:

"I perceived in those twenty minutes of cleared vision that in the youth of eternity we shall recapture that godlike capacity for endless enjoyment of the same thing which children possess, but which old age and the unreality of time have temporarily snatched from us."

Elsewhere she speaks of the after-effects of the experience as

"A release from disintegrating fear; a belief in the efficacy of suffering, and in the significance of mirth; a knowledge that love is the key with which to unlock the inner doors of life; an assurance that an Unseen Hand is guiding us; and a growing perception of beauty coupled with a thrilling apprehension of the mystery and ecstasy of life as being a vesture of the Holy Spirit."

Case 27 (Mrs. A.)

"It was a hot summer evening. I lay on the lawn in the back garden trying to get cool. The sun had almost set and I watched the planets appear. Suddenly I felt my head swelling. It seemed to increase in size until it contained the whole world: all the stars too. Everything that had ever happened or would happen was within myself. I was in my eighth year at the time, so knew little of history and nothing of religion. I saw many things, events I later learned about, also much I have as yet been unable to discover from any physical source. After what seemed untold ages I became aware of my mother telling me to come inside. There was a brief glimpse of my body lying on the grass with my mother bending over it. Then I was awake feeling very bewildered. It was some time before I recovered.

"After all these years I still refer to that experience whenever I want to verify anything I hear of or read about. There is always a sense that all happenings are right and in accordance with a plan. On several occasions since, the experience has been repeated on a smaller scale."

It seems probable that this was an out-of-the-body experience combined with mystical experience. The little girl of eight naïvely speaks of her "head swelling", which is obviously her way of expressing the sensation of expanded awareness.

Case 28

The last of the accounts which I shall present in this chapter came into my hands in an unusual way. I have a close friend who died in 1944. He was a man with outstanding qualities of mind and personality: he had wide interests, and among these (although known only to an intimate few) was mystical experience. Through the good offices of a sensitive he decided to make contact with me and did so about ten years after his passing over. I have subsequently put many questions to him and one of these concerned his progress on the mystic's path. What follows is part of an automatic script of this sensitive. The felicitous phrasing and the spirit of high adventure are very characteristic of the man I knew.

"Not long after my promotion to this life I prayed for a guide who should be master to the pupil and cause me to rise into the unitive life— attain to the mystical grade. My prayer was granted and because A. E. was of my time and generation on earth, but a little preceding me, he appeared radiant from the higher levels, and became my guardian philosopher.

"I will pass over the preparation, the conflict, the struggle, which were necessary to the creation of the inner harmony. I shall tell of my first experience which was an interpretation of a little corner of the earth, a vision, a feeling of the Unitive principle behind Nature in a small fragment of the world of the senses.

"It was an island in the Gulf of Mexico. There the winters are as mild as June in England. The sea about the island is as light and blue as a sapphire. I perceived green pastures, the earth crowned with fruits, groves of cedars, palms and oranges, brilliant but not cruelly burning sunshine that in the eyes of men apparelled Nature in its gayest colours. Life, swarming life in form is there. I had the sensuous human pleasure of perceiving it all. But how trivial was that pleasure when my mind gradually went inward to the genie. The process might be likened to that of a seagull on a cliff, with shut wings, just before its take-off from a jutting rock. Suddenly the great wings are outspread and it is off, rising, soaring above the immensities of the ocean beneath the wide cirrus-streaked skies. It is a poor simile, but how except objectively can I convey to you the ecstasy of that flight into Union. Then I knew the Unity behind the separate myriad forms animated by life on that small island. I was one with the Divine Imagining actively maintaining and conserving that fragment of Nature. I was one with the Artist experiencing the creative rapture which was his, one with the essence, the conception, and containing as well the physical representation, the imaged product of consciring. I was aware of the large, the little, the infinitesimal on that island. I experienced breath of life animating the tiniest coloured insect there; life in orange grove and cedar and tall waving palm; life in the black and white people on the isle; animal existence there. But it came like a chorus, many voices making one earth-time song. I was aware of the whole, of each separately, and of activating creative bliss.

"There is a quotation from the gospels I then truly apprehended—I have forgotten the exact words—'One sparrow shall not fall without your Heavenly Father knowing it'. How true that is when you, Raynor, realise that Divine Imagining maintains and conserves all Nature.

"That was my initial experience in this life of Transcendental Unity. It was a first lesson in mysticism for my liberated soul. I have had many other more wonderful experiences since: they were graded according to my progress. Beside me, fusing with me, always was my guardian philosopher, fusing at the peak, separate, instructing, guiding, as we climbed towards that peak.

"The first series of lessons concerned the planet Earth from which I had come. We traversed the Sahara deserts, we visited the poles, we absorbed the human life in great cities. We visited the lonely Himalayas, the Rockies. We went East, West, South, North, perceiving the outer, and then experiencing the inner in sections, the essence of each global section all preparatory to experiencing the life of Earth as one whole within Transcendental Unity. I have visited that secret country—Tibet's sacred centre, that other Northern spiritual centre, the dream island of Iona. I could write of all these mystical experiences—the peace, the enraptured quiet of the skies above Iona, the particular and the Whole of each centre.

"I rode upon the winds, rode over the waves, leaped the mountains, entered into the dewdrops of the dawn. I saw the conception of each in the essence, so much more exquisite, finer, subtilised. The initiatory conception is a country where beauty has no ebb, decay, no rotting, withering, where joy is wisdom, time an endless melody. Mistakenly I use the verb 'saw', but I experienced it within my whole being. A. E. and I have travelled the starry immensities . . . Some other time I may be permitted to tell you of further mystical heights and depths beyond all human knowledge."

COMMUNICATION AND COMMUNION

The significance of these experiences can only be appreciated if we have a conception of the existence of several different levels of communication between the self and the not-self. I have represented some of these in the neighbouring diagram which I shall expound without digressing to offer the evidence upon which it is based.

73

The diagram must not be taken for more than it is: an attempt to portray some levels of differing degrees of reality on which we may gather knowledge of the world. The upper half broadly corresponds to spiritual reality, the lower half to the levels of mind, and the lowest of the latter to our physical world. On the left-hand side of the diagram, the arrows represent the creation and maintenance of the external world to which we refer as Nature. On the right-hand side is an individual observer participating in these levels. As I have explained elsewhere,[1] the philosophic outlook known as Imaginism represents the Supreme Creator as least inadequately represented

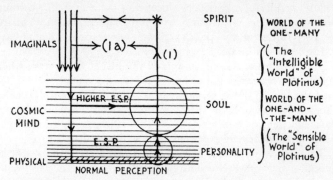

by the term *Divine Imagining*. The imaginals and a vast hierarchy of sub-imaginals are His modes or forms of imagining. They are the spiritual fountains, the primary sources of all that which lies behind manifested appearance. In this respect they are like the "Ideas" of Plato. Cosmic Mind is, as it were, a precipitate of Spirit having a lower degree of Reality than the latter. It is the instrument of Spirit by which the latter, in its diverse forms as "the Many", comes to know itself and evolve its latent potentialities. Using a simile of G. N. M. Tyrrell from the theatre, we might describe the Imaginals as the "author", Cosmic Mind as the "producer", and the physical levels as the "stage carpenter" of the world-drama. Undoubtedly many sub-levels of Mind may be recognised. A. E.,[2] writing of the creative process in a poet's mind, described three such strata:

"I was in some profundity of being. There was neither sight nor sound, but all was motion in deep being. Struggling desperately to remain there, I was being dragged down to the waking state, and then what was originally a motion in deep being broke into a dazzle of images which symbolised in

[1] *Nurslings of Immortality* (Hodder & Stoughton Ltd., 1957)
[2] *Song and Its Fountains*, p. 72 (Macmillan & Co. Ltd., 1932)

some dramatic way the motion of life in that profundity. And still being drawn down, there came a third state in which what was originally deep own-being, and after that images, was later translated into words. This experience I told to Yeats who said he had had an identical experience of the three states."

There may well be three or more such sub-levels of Cosmic Mind giving form to sub-imaginals on their way to precipitation in the physical world. Here I wish to draw attention to the probability that on several such levels there are forms of perception or modes of communication between the observing self and the world.

A lady, whose knowledge of these matters is considerable, has written to me as follows:

"With regard to seership, I am aware of three different ways of 'seeing'—etheric (?), mental, and spiritual.

"In the first, one sees apparently with the physical eyes what is not physically present. The seeing of what is known as the etheric or health aura is an example of this. As I have seen this, it consists of a pale-yellow or peach-coloured light round the head or shoulders. Rays can sometimes be discerned in it, radiating out strongly when the person is in good health, but when the person is ill or enfeebled the rays tend to droop.

"Another example of this was an experience that I had during the First World War. On waking up in the middle of the night, I saw before me a soldier standing on the side of a hill. The whole scene was some distance away so that I could not see distinctly enough to tell whether the soldier was British, French or German. Then a gun went off. I didn't 'hear' the shot, but was very conscious of its vibration. Then I saw clearly and vividly clouds of smoke arising which hid the hillside from my view. I waited until the last of the smoke had cleared away before switching on the electric light. This was to prove to myself that it was not a dream. I never heard anything afterwards to account for this vision, and have no idea why it should have been given to me. I can recall the scene almost as vividly today as I saw it all those years ago.

"In the second type of clairvoyance one sees, not with the eyes but with the mind. The mental pictures are of the same nature as those pictures of the imagination which one builds up consciously with the will, but in the case of clairvoyant seeing those pictures come unbidden. To give one example: one morning when I was sitting in my little shrine or meditation room, I became conscious of a monk standing in front on the right. He was young, and very gentle and benign-looking, and was dressed in a brownish tunic, lighter in colour than that of the Franciscans, and the rope round his waist was not white but of hemp. Though purely a mental seeing it was very vivid, and I should easily recognise him again.

"I had another experience of mental vision many years ago, soon after the First World War. It was in early January and I was in Edinburgh on the way to my work at the hospital. I could see a reddish sun, newly risen, against the frosty sky, and the clock on the church tower with the hands pointing at ten minutes to nine. Then suddenly, turning the corner of the street, I found myself in what appeared to be an underground temple in ancient Egypt. There was an altar in front of me, and a bearded white-robed priest stood behind the altar. On either side of me there were two rows of choristers chanting. I couldn't hear either the sounds or the words with my ears, but I heard them in a kind of inner way, mentally. I was conscious of rhythm and power. The group on my right chanted one line of the prayer or hymn while that on my left gave the response, and so on alternately. Meantime I was walking down towards the altar between them. Before I reached it the vision faded and I was back in twentieth-century Edinburgh. It dawned on me that it was about Osiris they were chanting, and in a flash I knew what it all meant. The words might have been taken out of our own service for Easter Day: 'As in Adam all die, even so in Christ shall all be made alive.'

"The third form of seeing might be called the mystic sense. It is a spiritual kind of vision and goes deeper, much deeper, than the mental. It arises through the awakening of the 'Spirit of Truth' in the deep hidden places of the soul—that spirit through which one can discern the Truth as it reveals itself to us from outside. It enables one to say, 'I see', 'I know', 'I am spirit: in my essential being I am at one with the Eternal, ageless and deathless, a thought in the Mind of God'. This is consciousness in the Eternal, in which the 'have been' and the 'shall be' are merged in the 'I am'."

If the reader will bring together the diagram on p. 74 and the poem used as introduction to this chapter, it will be observed that the first verse describes the familiar form of communication between the world and the self which we call visual perception. In the second verse, if by the "untroubled river" we understand the imaginal field, we have a description of the mystical experience of communion. The diagram illustrates how the "untroubled river" becomes a "second mind".

It is very important to distinguish true mystical experience from certain mental states which are sometimes described in language used of the former. The mental practice of one-pointed concentration on an object can lead to a state of so-called union of the mind and the object. From this state it is possible, I am told, either to regress into a negative mediumistic state or to enter a poised active state sometimes called contemplation.

We may also remind ourselves of a second quite different relationship of an observing mind to an object: it is one which is involved in object-reading or psychometry. Each object of the physical world has a field linked with it (sometimes called "etheric"), carrying a record of its past and future, and a sensitive mind may orientate itself towards the object in such a way as to become "one with" this field.

These two modes of orientation of an observing mind towards physical objects are mentioned here because we may easily forget them and suppose that normal perception is the only one to be considered. Their existence makes it necessary to be careful in affirming mystical union. Both one-ness and expansion may occur as phenomena of the *mental* level of the observer as well as in true mystical experience which is born of union with the imaginal field at a higher level. Where the lowest levels of mind are involved (often called the etheric levels) the phenomenon of union is called *participation mystique*. Something akin to an insulating membrane disappears and a mergence of the mental levels of the *personality* with the collective mind takes place. It gives a sense of expansion and unity, but the critical faculty has gone. In this submergence there persists a primitive type of communication which is characteristic of extra-sensory perception in primitive peoples. There is also, at this level, a primitive type of activity which is of the essence of magic.

On higher levels of mind the soul may also have experience of unity and expansion, but critical discernment is active now, and the experience is far removed from *participation mystique*.

With this theoretical framework we shall now consider the cases which have been presented.

COMMENTARY ON CASES 19 TO 28

In Case 19 I regard the "sense of identity with certain places in Nature" as on the level of the relationship found in object-reading or psychometry. The awareness of a "dimension which encompassed the spot" is probably a sensitivity to the etheric field carrying the past and future. There is no loss of the sense of "I". The reference to an increasing sense of the inter-relatedness of all things points to an ascent of awareness. The description which speaks of the "living-ness of nature", the sense of a "common texture of all things", and of the "inter-changeability of forms" suggests the rising of awareness above the lower levels, perhaps to the mid-mind levels—but it does not reach the higher levels of mind nor approach near the mystical level.

In Case 20 the brilliant descriptive power of Mr. Strong allows us to enter intimately into the experience. Expanded awareness moves about the mid-mind levels. Note that "human consciousness passed out from him, yet not into sleep; into no blurring of sense: something clear and shining". Here we have no *participation mystique* of the lower levels. The soul's awareness is able to move at will through a range of levels, rising at a high point to a "luminous sense of peace" and a "central unity of awareness". This was when the mind became quiescent, but as soon as the mind became active, "when the elated mind tried to realise it" or made "the effort to find words", the unity broke up "into a series of visions, creating multiplicity". This description is almost identical with A. E.'s experience (p. 74-5).

The closing part of the account refers to the light by which "he could illumine his own life and the lives of others" as slowly fading. He speaks of the legacy of "luminous wisdom and tranquillity" so that "for a few moments he knew that there was no human problem he could not solve". These features indicate a near approach of soul and Spirit, although short of union.

In Case 21 we have an account by another brilliant writer, Arthur Koestler. If it is compared in substance with the previous one, the agreement on all important points will be found complete. Thus, for example, Koestler writes, "The 'I' ceases to exist because it has, by a kind of mental osmosis, established communion with, and been dissolved in, the universal pool." Strong says that he "had seen the barrier broken down, relapsing through his special identity to the principle which he expressed, which all this coast expressed, affirming his union with it and its union with him". In differing phrases both speak of the peace, the perfection, the inter-relatedness of all things, and the luminous after-glow. It seems probable that both are close approaches to the mystical level.

Cases 22, 23 and 24 illustrate features we have already discussed and need no comment. In Case 25 the immediate experience is not described, but it seems clear that some measure of proximity of soul and Spirit persisted for several weeks. The effect of this upon ordinary living makes it a remarkable document. It is closely paralleled by an experience of Rabindranath Tagore which lasted seven or eight days. In similar terms he describes how a veil appeared to be withdrawn so that he was consciously and everywhere sensible of the glory and beauty of all things. "Everyone, even those who bored me, seemed to lose their outer barrier of personality; and I was full of gladness, full of love for every tiniest thing."[1] H. M. said, "Faces shone with serenity and a glowing loveliness; even the so-called ugliest was a picture of perfect beauty . . . Where, formerly, on every hand I had seen only the imperfections of my fellow-man, I saw now inherent nobility, purity, goodness and beauty, shining out and overshadowing the baser qualities". It was as if the soul in the near presence of the Spirit could see beyond each outer personality to the essential goodness within the other soul. Moreover, the new insight was not only into persons, it was also into truth. The brilliant and passionate account in Case 26 endorses these things also. M. P. M. says elsewhere, "In truth this life, here and now, is lovely enough to require no far-off heaven for its justification: because heaven, in all its spring-tide of beauty, is, here and now, surging up to our very feet, lapping against our heavy hearts, but we, alas, know not how to let it in!" To these we may add the testimony of Francis Thompson oft-repeated, as in his poem *The Kingdom of God* he deservedly rebukes us:

> The angels keep their ancient places;—
> Turn but a stone, and start a wing!
> 'Tis ye, 'tis your estranged faces,
> That miss the many-splendoured thing.

In a footnote Wilfrid Meynell adds, "For in these triumphing stanzas, he held in retrospect those days and nights of human dereliction he spent beside London's River, and in the shadow— but all radiance to him—of Charing Cross."

Case 28 is informative on several points. In a significant sentence he says, "I will pass over the preparation, the conflict, the struggle, which were necessary to the creation of the inner harmony". It is a reminder that the soul that would invoke its Spirit must prepare itself for that high privilege, as the great mystics have always realised. Nature-mysticism is clearly interpreted for us as being "one with the Divine Imagining actively maintaining and conserving that fragment of Nature". The experience was referred to in terms of a climb towards a mountain peak. As the less experienced mountaineer seeks the help of a guide, so on this high spiritual adventure two souls undertook the climb together. "Beside me, fusing with me, always was my guardian philosopher, fusing at the peak, separate, instructing,

[1] C. F. Andrews, *Letters to a Friend*, pp. 24–5 (George Allen & Unwin Ltd.)

guiding, as we climbed towards that peak." The account describes a series of experiences resulting in union with the imaginal activity sustaining different aspects of Earth. I draw attention to the description, "I was one with the Artist experiencing the creative rapture which was his, one with the essence, the conception, and containing as well the physical representation." The description may be directly applied to the left-hand side of the diagram (p. 74). It is as though standing above and within creation, he could look down on the precipitation of Divine Imagination from that country "where beauty has no ebb, where joy is wisdom, and time an endless melody", through successive levels of mind where it is given varied expression and forms until it rests finally in the substance of earth.

The unanimity of experience in all these varied accounts of different people in widely contrasting circumstances is an impressive thing. All things point to their source: a common principle, be it called Spirit, life, mind, or sentience, binds all things together.

> One grass-blade in its veins
> Wisdom's whole flood contains:
> Thereon my foundering mind
> Odyssean fate can find.[1]

[1] *The Works of Francis Thompson* (Macmillan & Co. Ltd.)

Chapter

5

DISCLOSURE OF THE NOT-SELF:
(II) OTHER SELVES

The fundamental fact of human existence is neither the individual as
such nor the aggregate as such. Each, considered by itself, is a mighty
abstraction. The individual is a fact of existence in so far as he steps into
a living relation with other individuals. The aggregate is a fact of existence
in so far as it is built up of living units of relation. The fundamental fact
of human existence is man with man.

MARTIN BUBER

IN this chapter we are concerned with the traverse (1b) of p. 28
where the near approach of Spirit to soul discloses profound significance in other selves. The theme is a continuance of that of the
preceding chapter. Case 27 recognises no gulf between communion
with Persons and Nature. Case 26 might well have been included
here, "I knew that every man, woman, bird and tree, every living
thing before me, was extravagantly beautiful, and extravagantly
important." In Case 24 J. P. W. wrote, "Nothing, nothing is excluded from the 'redemptive' process. Not only all men, but men
and rocks and stars and trees are brothers, are divine, and carry with
them the splendour awakening to Itself."

In one of the scripts of F. W. H. Myers written through the
sensitive Geraldine Cummins[1] there is the following passage:

"The Spirit of the Group-soul feeds with life and mental light certain
plants, trees, flowers, birds, insects, fish, beasts, men and women; repre-
sentatives of living creatures in varying states of evolution. It inspires
souls who are on various planes, various levels of consciousness in the
After-death. It feeds also creatures on other planets. For the Spirit must
gather a harvest of experience in every form. Gradually these intelligences
evolve and merge . . . You still exist as an individual; you are as a wave in
the sea."

Martin Buber, the well-known Jewish mystical philosopher, has
consistently stressed the importance of relationship and has written
a difficult book[2] on this theme. There is one idea central to his

[1] *The Road to Immortality* (Aquarian Press Ltd.)
[2] *I and Thou*, trs. R. G. Smith (T. & T. Clark Ltd., 1937)

outlook which I thought at first to be contradicted by the evidence
of mystical experience. He has emphasised the uniqueness of inter-
personal relationships which he expresses by the term I-Thou. He
has then pointed out the vast gulf between this and the relationship
between persons and things, which is symbolised by I-It. Indeed,
the latter is only in the technical sense called a relationship: it is an
attitude. At first, I thought that the gulf which Buber found between
them was contradicted by the evidence of mystical experience, for the
Nature mystics experienced a unity which embraced not only people
but rocks and trees and so-called inanimate Nature. Now I see that
the I-It attitude to Nature is commonplace, but it is not the mystic's.
The I-It attitude shouts at us when a man is regarded as a "hand"
by his employer, and not as a brother. It is of the very essence of
Nature-mysticism that it transforms the commonplace I-It attitude
to an I-Thou relationship. The mystic is mature in his relation to
men and mature in his relation to Nature, because he is wholly self-
giving to the Divine in both.

With these introductory remarks I present a few more accounts
of experience which ranges from levels of mind to near-mystical and
mystical communion. In Case 20, and others similar to it, contemplation of Nature led to the soul's increasing exaltation as its awareness
moved upward through mid-mind levels to a "luminous sense of
peace" and "a central unity of awareness". In Case 6 Olaf Stapledon
achieved a similar exaltation through contemplation of "being a self
in relation to other selves". It does not appear to matter which aspect
of the not-self engages the observer's attention. The important change
is *within the observer*. The soul's awareness is lifted towards the
Spirit—a process which may itself be initiated and guided by the
Spirit's descent towards the soul.

Case 29 (F. B.)

"Up to the age of 27 or so I met with frustration and difficulty both
in my private and professional life. At the age of 30 my sister, who was a
year younger than I, died after a lingering illness . . . Somehow after this
event I began to find myself more or less out of sympathy with my family—
father, mother and three brothers—and also with my friends. Certain
ideas and principles which I held were not shared by others, so that in
seeking closer companionship I met with little response or understanding
. . . I began to despair.

"One day, as I wandered in the fields near my home which was on the
border of Sherwood Forest, I became aware suddenly of a great change

in the landscape, especially in the sky, which appeared to be undergoing a kind of unfolding transformation, giving a vision of what appeared to be a shining host. This seemed to be real to me, although it is possible that my imagination may have contributed to the impression. At the same time everything around me took on a much more vivid, colourful and living appearance. The trees and flowers were friendly: they almost spoke to me. Here, before me, stretched out the Garden of Eden! The flow of water fascinated me, it was a miracle of leaping, dancing loveliness. This appearance around me continued, and the faces of people I now met, strangers and friends, were illumined. But how could I speak of 'strangers' now! Surely we were all one family, one living Unity! My feeling of estrangement, of being one apart from others, had gone. I had been living in a harsh world of conflict and misunderstanding; now here before me was my true home which I had always known, but in my blind ignorance had lost—the home to which I really belonged. I was humble and small in the presence of an Eternal Majesty, and yet I was elevated. I knew I could not trust my 'friends' who always betrayed me at one point or another; but they were all nevertheless loving creatures, and in some sense we all 'belonged together' . . . The memory of my vision of the 'Garden' has never left me. Now in my eighty-fourth year I find life peaceful and pleasant, and in spite of world-conflict, distressing as it is, I constantly give thanks for the wonder and joy of life.''

Case 30

This lady is a well-educated person. She was reading on a sofa, and had put down her book for a minute, as she said, "to try to visualise the fourth dimension as a projection of mind". She wrote:

"All at once I was conscious that the world had stopped, that there was an awful silence (i.e. full of awe), and I saw before me a sea of light into which I was about to plunge, but I hesitated on the brink. In that moment of consciousness I felt that if I proceeded into the light I might never return, or, if I did, I would never be the same again, and so I drew back, until the light died away and the world began to turn once more. It is difficult to explain these things in words for, though everything happens, nothing 'happens', and soon—all too soon—they 'fade into the light of common day'.''

This looks like the vision of a choice—the supreme choice—which she did not feel ready to make. The following experience of this lady is significant in the matter of personal relationships.

"There is a girl who has done me the greatest injury that one woman can do another, yet some higher power seemed to demand that I help this girl, even against my own will and my own material interests.

"We were standing one day talking earnestly, when I felt this sense of power and began to speak 'with authority'. I was in the doorway between two rooms; she was looking out at me, when suddenly she said, 'When you had your hair shampooed, did you have a blue rinse?' I thought this was rather a prosaic interruption to a serious conservation, but I replied: 'No, why do you ask?' She answered in a puzzled kind of way: 'Because there is a blue light round your hair, and it is beautiful.' I knew she was sensing the 'healing light'; we both became silent, the vibration grew more powerful, circulating between us, and in that moment I felt the compassion welling up in my heart, the forgiveness of Christ, the at-one-ment, and I knew that she felt it too, though she did not know what she felt. She flung her arms wide, her face upturned in a kind of ecstasy, while the tears poured down her cheeks, and she stammered: 'It's wonderful . . . it's marvellous, I . . .' What was working through me, I don't know, I can only guess, but I went and put my arms round her and said: 'It's all right,' and she replied: 'I have never felt so wonderful, so happy . . .' It affected us both profoundly.

"I know that when I have learned to feel true compassion for all humanity, as in that one moment of time, I shall enter the light without fear of hesitation, for then I shall *know* the time has come."

One hesitates to comment on so intimate an experience. In effect it seems to have been a rapport of two souls at mid-mind levels; but the operating power which worked behind must have been the Spirit—willing to draw near and lift two souls into ecstasy, when, through forgiveness, the barrier between them had been lowered.

Case 31 (M. W.)

The following incident occurred one winter night in Berkeley, California, during my student days:

"I was waiting for the train in a small waiting-room of the railway station. About fifteen or twenty other people were gathered there for the same purpose, all total strangers to me. Some were sitting reading newspapers or talking, and others stood huddling about a stove in the corner of the room. There was the usual subdued chatter of voices with occasional laughter. It was a familiar, rather a commonplace scene.

"Suddenly, I was aware of some mysterious current of force, subtle, yet of unimagined potency, which seemed to sweep through that small drab waiting-room. A kind of glory descended upon the gathered company—or so it seemed to me. I looked at the faces of those around me and they seemed to be suffused with an inner radiance. I experienced in that moment a sense of profoundest kinship with each and every person there. I loved them all!—but with a kind of love I had never felt before. It was an all-embracing emotion, which bound us together indissolubly in a deep unity of being. I lost all sense of personal identity then. These people were no longer strangers to me. I *knew* them all. We were no longer separate individuals, each enclosed in his own private world, divided by all the barriers of social convention and personal exclusiveness. We were one with each other and with the Life which we all lived in common. I think in this moment I understood for the first time the meaning of those words 'the mystic brotherhood'.

"This whole experience must have only lasted for a matter of moments —for soon the train arrived, we all dispersed—and the power and the glory fled! I felt its aftermath for a long time, however, and often pondered it in my memory. I am sure that it was a purely subjective experience on my part. At least I had no way of ascertaining that it was otherwise. I shall never know whether any of those others present at the time shared my vision, or sensed the descent of the Dove in that little rail-road station."

Observe how with the drawing-near of the Spirit, the soul breathes a new atmosphere, for which our word "love", even at its highest, seems too small.

Sir Francis Younghusband in his book *Heart of Nature*[1] wrote of an experience which had once come to him:

"I had a curious sense of being literally in love with the world. There is no other way in which I can express what I then felt. I felt as if I could hardly contain myself for the love which was bursting within me. It seemed as if the world itself were nothing but love . . . At the back and foundation of things I was certain was love—and not merely placid benevolence, but active, fervent, devoted love, and nothing less. The whole world seemed in a blaze of love, and men's hearts were burning to be in touch with one another."

Ellis McTaggart the Cambridge philosopher, writing to Younghusband, said, "It is a great help and comfort to know that people feel the same as oneself, especially to find that a man, whose outward life has been so very different from mine as yours has been, has found his way to the same inner reality." [2]

In Thomas Burke's book *The Wind and the Rain*[3] the author gives an account of an experience which came to him in a London slum:

[1] Published by John Murray Ltd., London
[2] G. Lowes Dickinson, *McTaggart* (C.U.P., 1931)
[3] Published by Thornton Butterworth Ltd.

Case 32

"Then I heard the jingle of an organ playing the 'Hiawatha' cake-walk, and as I plodded towards it I reached the entry of a court. There, in the court itself, I saw the organ, and around it I saw a group of ragged girls, kicking up black mud to its Bacchic rhythm. The cobweb daylight that entered the court from above illuminated only the faces and tangled hair of the dancers, and feet and bodies could hardly be seen. For the first time that day I halted, and stood and watched them. Now they went slowly in mock tragedy, and now they went furiously, and now they screamed . . . In my weak and dazed condition I felt ready to plunge into the mud and roll in it with them. As the dance and the cries of the crowd grew more furious, a window on the first floor was thrown up, and into the grey light came a lean pale face; a face with eyes wide and lips parted in a chuckle; an ugly spectacle meeting my own ugliness. And suddenly, as I leaned exhausted against a post, came one of the moments of my life. In that moment I was conscious of time arrested and of the feeling that I was looking on a picture as old as the world; and that those tattered children, that gloating face and myself were and had been part of it. And into the thick of my desolation came a glow of exaltation. I was aware of strength and clearness. I felt capable of anything. The most difficult achievement seemed possible to me. I longed then and there for pencil and paper that I might try again to write the tale of Quong Lee's window and of his court. Then the moment was gone."

It was not perhaps a profound experience: the timeless moment was experienced on mid-mind levels rather than beyond them. But here is Burke's philosophy of life:

"Each man's city of refuge must be built within himself—of broken toys. The only people who truly live are those who are always beginning again. It was not I who mattered, but love itself; not my suffering that must be eased, but love that must be served. *Only by love do we come to understanding and truth.* The mocking magic that comes and goes is the lamp that is lighting us to beauty. The beauty is the happiness of God, and is not in clouds or on hilltops, but everywhere about us."

It is an exciting and deeply moving thought that to the eye of the soul, when the Spirit draws near, the ugliness of appearance is lost in the essential Beauty, the stains of personality are obscured by the all-pervading love of the One, and that in a wretched slum or murky alley one may be a Watcher on the Hills—the fresh green hills of the Spirit.

The last account which I shall present in this chapter is written

X by a thoughtful young mother, whose working day, with four children, is full of household duties and cares. The writer has aimed at accuracy and used words carefully. It reaches up to the brink of mystical experience along the path of completely unselfish love and prayer—the traditional way of the Christian saints—and it does so in an ordinary domestic environment. She says modestly, "I confess that I am not practical or efficient at my work, despite my earnest endeavour to combine a contemplative attitude to life with performance of the many duties involved in the living of it."

Case 33 (Mrs. D. E.)

"For a long time I had been asking, what is it that motivates human behaviour? I recognised that I needed the security of self-esteem to compensate for certain feelings of inferiority within me. It seemed apparent that all people were fundamentally the same, i.e. in desperate need of security, or belonging as a vital unit in the physical visible world. This was no original idea in that thousands had already reached the same conclusion, but it was for me an idea which did originate in my own mind.

"From that point, I looked at all my actions and thinking, refusing to dwell upon this or that, except briefly for practical reasons, because it seemed a false way of achieving security and happiness.

"I thought of God as the sum total of all the love in the world but did not altogether endow Him with a personality. Many years before, I had decided that my love of truth would permit me to accept nothing unless it was clear to me. I felt there must be a point where the love of God ceased to be words and became experience, and did sometimes feel that I had touched upon that experience in part.

"Then, a dramatic period arose when a friend was in great distress of mind. More than anything else she needed love and understanding. Her family, through no fault of their own, were unable to supply it. I could not see ahead very far, and yet I was willing to serve God. God became a tremendous source, in fact the only source, of love and strength and understanding. The whole period is a complete vital story on its own.

"For that space of time I gave up all thoughts of myself, in practical help and earnest prayer. Prayer had a deep new meaning. Where I was conscious of myself at all I knew that I was perfectly relaxed, had no fears, and had a sense of being filled with what I shall call the peace of God. I had no time to think of my own needs and yet I was aware that somewhere within this framework was the perfect security I had been searching for.

"My friend turned to me for security and strength, and then, from no other source but God's guidance, re-established her purpose for living. Her family's hurt pride and resentment made them antagonistic towards me. Their utter blindness to the wonderful evidence of God's love made me wonder if, after all, my new-found peace and confidence were not based upon some horrible mistake.

"My doubts now made the future appear blank, dark and meaningless. I knew with all my being that I would never find God at any time, if this path of love did not lead to Him. I had to summon up my courage and force myself to ask: had this giving out of selfless love been not from God at all, but merely a cunning device of my own to satisfy that fundamental need for self-esteem? If this was so, then the inescapable conclusion seemed to be that there was no God, no purpose, nothing to cling to, hope for, or trust.

"One night, the antagonism and lack of understanding on the part of my friend's family, together with a combination of other unhappy circumstances, led me to feel unloved, unimportant and altogether alone. I was tempted imaginatively to construct circumstances to justify myself, but stopped and would not permit myself even this last frightened attempt at regaining my self-esteem and security.

"Quite suddenly at this point, and quite without any anticipation, some part of me—I shall call it my mind—was hovering uncertainly, apparently above my body. I was taken unawares; I became desperately frightened. 'Where did I possibly go wrong in my thinking?' I cried out to myself. 'Always along the way I have travelled in my thinking, I have only wanted to find the truth and to serve God.'

"I cannot describe my terrible fear and the darkness and confusion and insecurity which confronted me. The loneliness in my own mind was terrifying and very real. It is not an exaggeration to say that I felt I must be on the brink of insanity. 'I must hang on and think calmly and quietly, and I will find a way back to peace and security,' I told myself in the midst of my fear.

"Looking back upon the experience, I know that I have gained a depth of insight and an understanding of behaviour that I would not have had otherwise. I could so easily have directed my thinking to an object or an idea or a person and clung to it, but would not. I longed to find my security in something that could be trusted utterly to be permanent, eternal and indestructible.

"Up to that time I had not considered what vital part Jesus had to play except that He was filled with the love of God. I had neither agreed nor disagreed with orthodox teaching, although I had thought a great deal about it. At that moment, however, I began to feel that Jesus would show me the next step, that I could trust in His recorded teachings to find the peace I needed. (I had always thought of Him as Christ before, never particularly as Jesus. There could be another simple explanation, but to me it was as if the name of Jesus was presented to me from somewhere outside the range of my own thinking.) I also felt, unmistakably, 'This is what Jesus went through in His search for truth.'

"My next impression was no vision but simply a crystal clear form of thinking which I knew to be the truth. I could see humanity as so many individual spirits, all progressing towards God. They were united, but did not know it. Those who could just catch a glimpse of the truth put out a loving hand to lift up and support the fallen, and these same sometimes fell themselves and were lifted up in their turn. I observed all this not from outside humanity, but as it were from within. There was a thrill and a certainty in being included, or rather in knowing that exclusion could not possibly be. (My choice of words dissatisfies me—they are so inadequate.)

"It seemed so clear that God must have created us out of love in order that the free spirits of men might intermingle and unite ultimately in one glorious God-filled loving fellowship.

"I accepted as the truth that to think, not of myself, but of the others who were all part of the same great whole, was to commence upon the fulfilment of God's purpose. It was to me the beginning of wisdom.

"I quietly turned all the energies of my mind away from myself towards my husband and my children, and as I did so I discovered within myself a tremendous capacity for selfless love that I had not known existed.[1] A deep peace and happiness wiped out the terrible fear. In the next few days I often remembered my experience, and the memory could set my heart pounding and every nerve tense with fear, but always I turned from myself to loving and praying for others, and always instantly found peace.

"At this stage I did not accept fully Christ's actual presence although I somehow felt that in thinking of Jesus so unexpectedly and finding something there to cling to for safety, the suggestion came from Jesus Himself. To accept His loving presence seemed the next obvious step to take, and at the instant I began to do so in faith and trust, an indescribable peace and presence began to fill me. Instantly, I drew back. Here were all my doubts again. 'Am I only trying to escape from my fear? Am I only pretending that Jesus is here, for my own sake? Is it only fear of insecurity that makes me tell myself that I love all people?' I knew that I could not really escape from this frightening position except by finding the truth in unmistakable terms.

"On the following Sunday I attended my usual church service. In the middle of the sermon came this: 'There is an outpouring of love and sympathy towards others which takes no thought for itself. This love is not to make one feel good. It is selfless and is from God Himself.' The immensity of the implications in these few sentences brought quiet tears to my eyes. I learned later that these words were not planned by the

---

[1] In all the months that have passed since this period I am describing, I have never been able to fill my mind with this love simply in order to feel that way. It has always gone hand in hand with a sense of my own insufficiency.

speaker. He told me, 'I had no idea why I made such a point of this except to say that God inspired me to do so.' "

"Whether this man understood fully what was involved in my experience but thought that I did not, or whether he understood only in part, I do not know, but he gave me the very advice, indeed, the only advice that could have been of any help to me, namely—'You are in a frightening position where you cannot go back, and yet to go forward you must take a leap of faith into the darkness and believe utterly that God is there and that you will find Him.'

"That leap of faith was not made instantaneously. It was quiet, unhurried and free. In the weeks that followed, I found the greatest contentment, strength and happiness, and also the best health I have ever had.

"One night I was settling down for sleep with my body quite relaxed. I turned to my loving prayer for my family, and forgot myself more completely than I have ever done before. I was completely filled with love, in which no thought of myself entered at all. A great wave or cloud swept over me. I left my body behind. I could hear it breathing deeply and evenly on the bed below. Still with this tremendous love enveloping me, I turned to *my* God (and here I choose the words with great care) in *purity*, *trust*, *reverence*, and a *soul-expanding worship*. In that instant a great light or radiance was present, such light as I had never seen before. It was not a light that I saw with my eyes. Momentarily, I was prepared to continue my trust in God, and the transforming radiance was about to unite with my very being, to become part of my real self or soul. I knew that to give myself utterly to God was to change my personality absolutely and for ever: it would be to relinquish my 'self'.

"I doubted God's judgment. 'What if I am dead or about to die? I am not afraid, but this is too unexpected and strange. I must have time to think about it and decide what it means. I know that here is the Truth. But I must look after my children. I must retain my free self to direct my life and theirs.' Also involved in my hesitation was the fear that God might lead me into embarrassing situations. Even while I hesitated the radiance receded, and I returned to my instantly wide-awake body with inexhaustible matter for the deepest thought.

"I tell myself now that I should have trusted God completely, that it should have been His will to say whether I should live or die, continue my life as formerly or completely change my ways of living. I know now that I was not near to death at all, only closest to the richest spiritual experience possible. In the days that followed this, I felt that God continued to be with me. Yet deep within me, I knew that I had held back from giving myself to Him wholly and unreservedly.

"I gradually came to realise that the human personality comprised two distinct parts. Our real 'selves' consisted of an indestructible spiritual identity, and our lower physical, emotionally-controlled selves were governed by our apparent security or insecurity in the physical world. In my moment of choice, I could have been freed from this lower half of my personality. I rested quietly in the knowledge that God understood my inability to accept Him simply and unquestioningly. I constantly asked of myself, 'Did God mean us to reach this stage of freedom in this life? Was it only a glimpse of the beauty, wonder and purposefulness of life after death when we should have left our physical selves behind, that God had given me?'

"There was one moment when I caught a glimpse of how all the lives of all people are intertwined, and how the insecurities of one individual, and the aims, interests and forms of security adopted, leave their indelible mark upon all those who come into contact either directly or indirectly with him. The inability of even one person to grasp the significance of spiritual truth and its path to freedom contributed to a similar inability in others.

"This picture was so immense in its sorrow and pathos that I felt myself reaching out into all the lives of the people surrounding me, loving them yet weighted down with sadness at their blindness, longing to show the reality and beauty and love of God to them, yet frustrated by the inevitability of their imprisonment by their physical senses. The magnitude of all this underlying life seemed to make my mind expand, but in such a way that I could not cope with it. I prayed, 'Lord, don't let me think any more just now. It is far too big for me.' I halted my thinking on the brink of vast knowledge, feeling too child-like and inadequate for the attendant intolerable sadness and yearning.

"In an infinitesimal way I had seen into God's wonderful plan for us, and our ultimate union with Him, and in my impatience I longed for humanity to find a quick and easy way to fulfilment. Yet it was forced upon me to admit that God's way was the only way. For us finally to become one with God we clearly must begin in a physical world. Our spirits could launch out on their long eternal journey only from a state of being akin to childhood. In sudden wonder, I saw that in the infinity of this unending reality I was simply a little child.

"I looked at the fear, suffering and perplexity in the world, and knew that just as wise parents do not despair at the childishness of their children, so God does not despair over us. He does not need to, since He can already see us arriving at our final goal after our long ages of experience. In a truer sense, we are already in a state of being contained within God, never having been out of it, but in our immaturity, i.e. our continual desperate turning to a thousand things for security, we are incapable of consciously grasping it. (Words are so hopelessly inadequate.) God is patient because He is outside the dimension of time. There is a deep, deep, thrill and joy for me in this conviction of His 'timelessness' and 'patience'. I am not just borrowing another's word, but it is well-nigh impossible to describe how this patience became part of me. During these weeks, *time* had a different quality. I am not suggesting that I could see more events over a greater span of time than ordinarily. The 'past' and the 'future' did not matter greatly. It was living so entirely in the present that gave me such perfect health.

"How did all this apply to the conduct of my home and the needs of my children? One thing stood out clearly. It was God's purpose that I should live my life not for my own satisfactions, but for love of others. 'Love of others' was not to be a sentimentality, but was to embrace practicality on the physical level, appreciation of spiritual needs, and discrimination between courses of action designed to advance or impede progress towards God. To set out on this road every day brought the deepest sense of purpose, but simultaneously, awareness of my own baffling ignorance and utter insignificance in my own strength. I desperately needed God's guidance. I felt now that I wanted to submit my will entirely so that God could guide me.

"On one occasion I felt particularly helpless. It was not a dramatic situation by the usual standards. My two sons, aged ten and eight, were quarrelling in the adjacent room. It was a typically childish argument over a trifle, but I felt part of me rising up in annoyance and impatience. I was tired after a long day. My three-year old daughter was sitting at the table repeatedly refusing to eat her dinner. My husband, perhaps with some justification, not apparent to me at the time, gruffly demanded his customary but hitherto overlooked cup of tea! The boys began to endanger themselves with their fighting. In that instant I knew that the irritability of the lower half of my personality would explode into a disproportionately angry outburst. Even as I walked towards the boys with my hands raised ready to thrust them apart roughly, I cried out to my God in my heart. (I cannot describe my earnestness simply as prayer—it was so very much a cry to God. It was actually wordless, a rapid thinking experience without the use of words—but I cannot convey that to paper.) As nearly as I can describe it my approach to God was, 'Lord, I love them. I do not want to hurt them. Left to myself I am helpless. Help me, my God! I freely submit my will, my mind, everything that is in me—for their sakes!'

"As I arrived at the spot where the boys stood, I found that it was not I who acted at all. I felt that some power other than myself controlled me, but it was a power of love which could be trusted. My hands were gentle as I separated the combatants—I could feel the love flowing out towards them—and they instantly clung one to each side of me, both smiling lovingly and happily up at me. In their eyes was a simple trust that I have never seen in them before or since. If I attempted to explain what happened I could only suggest that the tremendous love surging out from me flowed unhindered into their simple and uncluttered child-minds.

"I then turned to the baby and spoke to her. It was as if it were not I who determined what words were to be spoken. I do not even remember what they were. I do know, however, that my voice was gentle, and that the little one picked up her spoon and began to eat contentedly. I turned to my husband and found him quietly preparing the tea.

"For the brief space of time here outlined, I was an entirely different personality. There was no 'self' demanding attention. It was as if all of me were outgoing. But more than that, the most vivid impression was that my will had disappeared. And yet I was free. Slowly, but deliberately and freely, I withdrew from the unexpected situation, and resumed my more familiar 'normal' personality.

"Then my questioning began. 'Did God mean human personality to arrive at this point? Is this what God meant us to be like? Is this the logical outcome of faith, trust and submission to God? Do I really want to continue with my "self" relinquished?'

"A few days later, I was listening to a devotional session on the radio. The speaker posed the question of the Christian's attitude to war. This question seemed very important. Thousands of better thinkers than I had dealt with this problem of war, and yet I felt so sure that God was with me that I sat down to think about it, fully expecting to arrive at a conclusion.

"I do not write these last paragraphs with assuredness. At the time it all seemed so clear and simple, but up to this present moment I am still analysing the whole experience, and holding it up to myself for criticism. I shall describe it and the preliminary line of thought, just as they were.

"This love of God within me was for all humanity. Prayer for those I loved seemed to be a projection of God's love from my 'real self' along a connecting channel which was 'God-inclusive-of-other-selves' to the deep levels of the mind or the 'real self' of the person for whom I was praying. To pray for an enemy would therefore be to pour God's love into a mind— that mind being bent on destruction. To such a mind the result would surely be confusion. Would not a nation-wide loving united prayer for the enemy avert war by God's very own means and power placed at our disposal? It would be naïve, indeed, to suppose that any so-called 'Christian' nation at its present stage of development could attain to such an ideal. To a God-loving individual, however, who felt it (even if mistakenly) to be God's way, it would become in fact the only tenable inner approach to war. At that particular time, the world-situation was very tense. Russia was a threat to the Middle East. As I sat there, I became convinced that there was a high-ranking Russian whose mind I could reach with prayer. I had an impression vaguely visual of an actual man, for whom I experienced a great compassion and love. It did not simply come upon me. I did in fact freely direct myself to feel this great love for this man. Every energy of my mind was earnestly directed to transmitting this deep love and compassion which was of God along the channel connecting the deep levels of our minds, and believing utterly that God was involved, and that what I was imagining (if you will) was actually taking place.

"I felt 'myself' travelling along this channel, and then knew that I was separated from my body. It was an experience of freedom. My real self was not imprisoned in the physical world at all! I was wide-awake and alert. Nothing that could happen to my physical body, even death itself, could possibly touch me or harm me. I deliberately moved my hands and arms just to see if I could, and stood up and walked across the room. In the instant of separation, I forgot about the Russian in the beauty and wonder of the experience. It was as if a pure, fully-conscious self was freed, and all fears, insecurities, impulses and sins (using the word as I understand it) were left behind. There was no fear, but the strangeness, of the experience prompted me to pray, 'Lord, my Lord Jesus, be with me.' I walked the length of the house, spoke to my little daughter, with my voice and manner unusually gentle and kind. At this point I crept back (speaking figuratively) into the more familiar surroundings of my body.

"Up to the present moment, I have not found satisfactory answers to my many questions. Can the earnestness of loving prayer be measured in terms of the depth of entry into the spiritual planes of existence? Similarly, is the effectiveness of prayer relative to the same? Should loving prayer for another necessarily result in this leaving the physical world behind? How earnestly should we pray?

"I cannot conceive of a God who says, 'Thus far shall you love and pray for another, and no farther.' *My* God is boundless, infinite, and inexhaustible in His love.

"I can see the similarity, in its beginning, between this experience and the previously described one involving the transforming radiance and light. The difference partly lies in the fact that upon the first occasion I continued in selflessness and purity and love to soar up towards communion with God, whereas on the second occasion I was very much aware of myself in a strange situation, and therefore I lost hold of the beauty of this selfless love."

This way of life is called by the Indian saints Bhakti Yoga. Its Christian formulation is expressed in St. John's words, "God is Love; and he that dwelleth in Love dwelleth in God, and God in him." I cannot avoid a strong feeling that it is such love, poured quietly and selflessly into the turgid stream of human affairs by both cloistered and domestic saints, which counteracts the toxins which society is always generating; that it is this, indeed, which prevents our world from running to destruction, and which will perhaps ultimately achieve its redemption.

When scientists have found the way to Nature's last secrets, when philosophers have come to agreement, when statesmen have founded a world government, and theologians are humble before the mystery of Being—the loving soul will still compel our tribute of awe and reverence—the praise of the gods and the noblest achievement of mankind.

Chapter

6

HIGHER MYSTICAL EXPERIENCE

Or if I reach unusual height
Till near His presence brought,
There floods of glory check my flight,
Cramp the bold pinions of my wit,
    And all untune my thought;
Plunged in a sea of light I roll,
Where wisdom, justice, mercy, shines;
Infinite rays in crossing lines
Beat thick confusion on my sight, and overwhelm my soul.

Great God! behold my reason lies
Adoring: yet my love would rise
    On pinions not her own:
Faith shall direct her humble flight,
Through all the trackless seas of light,
To Thee, th' Eternal Fair, the infinite Unknown.

ISAAC WATTS

THE accounts of mystical experience in previous chapters have all dealt with a transient experience, although its after-effects on the recipient may have been profound. In a few cases, of which 25 is an example, a near-Illuminative state lasted several weeks. But in no case could the subject re-enter that state at will, or hold permanently the union of soul and Spirit. Is this possible? The answer, which seems to be "Yes", would take us into a study of the classical mystics, men and women whose surrendered lives were fully devoted to this supreme quest of the soul. We shall say a little of their methods in Chapters 8 and 10. A mystic writes, "In the Unity of the Spirit we are freely *held*: as long as we have to hold we are not fully united."

Apart from establishing a *permanent* close degree of union of the soul with the Spirit of its Group-soul, is any higher mystical experience recorded? The chief difficulty in forming an opinion resides in the limitations of language; but there is evidence in two cases, which I present below, of the perception of still higher levels of Reality.

The following account is contributed by the person whose childhood experience was given in Case 2. There is described, first, an experience of Illumination or near-Illumination which might be called permanent. The account has been a little condensed. It is a moving human story—the spiritual Odyssey of a courageous woman who put this prolonged state to some severe tests and found that it validated itself. After this came gleams of something higher still.

Case 34 (X. Y.)

"*The Living Light.* For three years previously to 1920 I was hemmed in by a black darkness—of my own making—so it seemed to me then. Then I was invaded by a great Light which swept away that darkness. It soaked me with the goodness of God, and I could *see* in that Light, that that goodness must be the hidden life of every human being.

"This was not a brief experience like the child's. It went on for months, even years, and occurred intermittently for a long time after when I attended. I am of a sceptical turn of mind, and that part of me wanted to test it out in my own experience, to see if it really was true in the world around. I decided to give up teaching and go and do housework for someone who needed it and couldn't afford help.

"My people would have worried had they known what I had in mind. So I said I would go for a holiday to my cousin at W——, who lived in a religious community. I had seen little of her, and knew nothing of community life, nor even of ordinary church services. I hoped she would understand what was being shown to me in this Living Light.

"As I was carrying my suit-case downstairs to be ready to go next morning, someone came and asked if I would take over a little school for six weeks while her sister was having an operation. I did, and six weeks or so later I set out for W——, arriving there just before Easter. After a time there I told my cousin what I had in mind, about going on from there to help poor mothers with children. She said if I felt this need to do manual work, there was plenty I could do there, after I had had a free time to think and rest. She suggested my staying there for the summer term. The sisters all took part in some house duties. The Mother did the supper washing-up for about a hundred and forty.

"I helped in various ways outside and in; it was one of the most carefree periods of my life. I enjoyed every minute of it, except that I knew I had to go on with the purpose for which I had come.

"After four months, or more, there, I set out on foot with a little money for lodgings. The first night I had supper, bed and breakfast at an inn for three and sixpence. Next night I was offered a free night's lodging by a miner's wife who saw me walking up and down the streets to find one. It was a four-roomed house and sheltered grandfather and grandmother, a child of about ten, two lodgers and the mother of the child. I slept with her in the front room, in a bed drawn out of a cupboard. The young woman washed in the room where the lodgers were having breakfast. They took no notice of her. I only washed my face! They thought

I must be in trouble and gave me a shilling to get a tram-ride. A baker gave me a lift in his bread cart also.

"On the third evening I reached a town where I asked for a bed and breakfast at a hostel until I could get a job. They told me where I could get cheaper lodgings, but let me stay there. There was a bath there, thank goodness! They had no idea how to help me into a job such as I was after. They told me they thought I must be doing it for a bet, or to write about it. They looked down on domestic work, or, rather, on those who did it.

"During the next days I walked miles trying to get this job, where I could serve the goodness of God hidden in a needy soul—without success, as I could give no references to a servants' registry.

"There was an advertisement in a local paper for a housekeeper for a miner, a widower with two children. I walked twelve miles there as I had spent my money. A row of dismal miners' houses—two rooms down, an iron staircase and two rooms up; occupied, I found, by two families; no gardens. I knocked at the front door. A girl of nine or ten opened the door, leading straight into a room with a double-bed in which a youth was sleeping. I should have gone round to the back. She took me into the other room, hot and dusty with a fire in August—with a double-bed almost touching it. There was a small window and a table by the back door. A rough bearded old man greeted me. I could not understand his dialect, nor he me. The child interpreted each to the other. The men came in by the back door when returning from night or day shifts, but he said they never looked at folks in bed. I was to sleep with the child in this room, the fire being kept in all night for washing and drinking. Could I wash, bake, etc., etc.? After many questions he said I'd do and embraced me. I did not like this and said so. It wasn't easy to discern the beauty of holiness in him, but he said he wouldn't do it again. I can still recall the thoughts that flashed through me. He sent the girl, I think, to get a shilling. He said he was playing this week, which meant he wasn't working. He put it in my hand to seal the bargain, and asked if I would stay there and then. He told me to help myself from the pot of tea on the hob, and told the child to go and get a loaf. They were arguing about something. She wouldn't go without the money, so I pushed the shilling across the table for her to take for the bread. She returned with a big loaf. He told me to help myself. There was no milk nor butter. I was hungry and glad to eat some bread, but the tea still remained in the cup when the postman arrived with, I should say, forty to fifty letters. He opened them one after the other. All were applications for the job. He couldn't read and asked me to read them to him. Then there was a knock at the front door. The girl fetched him into the other room. There was whispered talk for some time before he returned.

"He told me straight away it was 'a widow who speaks our language. She wants to come and settle in now. Five shillings a week she wants, and she knows our ways.' But as he had given me his shilling, he said he could not say yes to her. Would I mind if he had her instead of me?

"I had never dreamed of all these women wanting to take such a job. I hadn't refused it, but I couldn't take it now, could I? So with heart-felt relief I accepted this dismissal. 'But you must take the shilling,' he said. And I was glad to have it to pay the bus fare back to the hostel instead of walking twelve miles. I returned it later, when I succeeded in getting a job in a family of four young children under school age.

"This job with the family of four children was waiting for me on my return to the hostel. I was told to go to their address. The mother looked askance at me, without references. The baby reached out her arms to me to come to me. 'That decided me,' the mother told me afterwards. It was a temporary job, but could have become permanent. Next, I looked after a mentally and physically afflicted old woman. One mother thought I was 'in trouble', but took me because of her own great need . . . Then I heard that my grandfather had died and my aunt was alone and mentally sick. I went to live with her. (Charity begins and ends at home.)

"This may sound a silly reaction to you. To match the radiant joy of this Living Light, I just had to take on what seemed joyless, or with little joy in it. Through it all, and for years after, this Living Light was still with me, but interwoven with deeper qualities. The years with my aunt tested it most of all. That this Living Light was no wishful thinking was manifested most clearly then.

"The Light possessed me. I lived in IT and with IT pervading all these varied relationships with strangers and my aunt. It spilled over all around. In my being, I needed no proof. It drove me to do all these things. It was no neurotic compulsion. It was fullness of Light and Life such as I had never before known. It made me want to turn daily work into worship.

"*The Dark, Hidden One*. Daily living went on. Dark problems and difficulties were lit up by that penetrating Light. One had a growing consciousness of interweaving relationships, in and out of, and within, these realms of spiritual life, which streamed into the living and hard physical work. (It was no joke to be living day after day with one who was mentally and spiritually sick, and strong physically.)

"Then about 1924 came a period when it was Dark—not the darkness of despair, nor of evil. (I had known that.) But a fuller, deeper Life than that of Spirit, mighty as that is. It was dark to the understanding. It did not cut out the Light that had been with me for the last four years. It wove into that, and attracted—compelled—the attention beyond the Light. It was awesome in its hidden majesty—a Power so full and terrible in its manifoldness—something wholly *Other* than I had before been brought up against.

"There was a terrible loneliness with it. I longed to meet someone who could explain, and help me to meet it. There was no one I knew of. It is hard at the best to find courage to speak of such an experience, going on

99

day after day, week after week. People could so easily assume I was 'imagining things'. I sought help in books. Dean Inge's book on Plotinus came my way. I knew quite well from experience that the living 'Ideas' he wrote about are all beyond all conceptual thought. I recognised the impossibility of converting what—WHAT—was before me into human thought-forms. Concepts—as we regard them nowadays—are mere sediment from this teeming dark Life whence creative Ideas and 'archetypal images' stream forth. I was desperate to find someone who could understand. Perhaps Inge did; but I did not find it there. It may have been there, but I missed it at the time.

"Something I had read ten years or so earlier came to me: the story in the Bhagavad Gita of Arjuna's sight of the Universal Form (the eleventh chapter). I do not mean that any imagery like that which Arjuna saw came into my mind—much less hallucinations. His description repelled me ten years ago. It does now. Only now, I could understand that—behind the Gita's horrible imagery of the manifoldness and otherness of the divine creativeness weaving through the universe—Arjuna was aware of a central Rest that is undisturbed by all its breathing in and out through the Cosmos and its multitudinous Beings. 'Forgive us, O Home of the Universe, that we have dared to call you "Friend".'

"That was the nearest I had come across. Later, I found such an experience hinted at, under other imagery, by Western Christian mystics.

"Yes, God hidden in the very depths of our beings. He is also so wholly *Other* that we cannot grasp the workings of His thoughts. His Beauty and Power and Wholeness are so above-earthly that it seems no beauty that we could desire It. Yet, this unrefracted Beauty, claims one's love far more powerfully than the shining manifest Goodness, which had been playing through my life for some years.

"This, I saw, is the hidden God whom people worshipped in church and chapel. As far as I could remember, I had not felt the need of joining with the others in worship. Now, I did. I knew at first hand what naked worship is. I could no longer stay alone confronted—permeated—by this Divine Darkness. I must belong to some fellowship of worshippers.

"Whom? I knew something of Methodist services, with their hearty singing and preaching. I wanted to be quiet to worship the Wholeness of Majesty.

"I knew something of Quaker worship. Their silence appealed to me personally. But I felt in my bones that it must be a fellowship of all sorts of folk: and silence would hang heavily on many.

"What about the Roman Catholic Church? No. Judged from the outside the Church of England seemed the happy mean. I had not attended ordinary service there, but I knew that confirmation was the gateway into it. My mind settled on that.

"The next step? There was no church in our village. I had never seen the old vicar of the nearest church. I did not like to go and ask him about it. I decided to go to my cousin who was a sister in an Anglican community, to seek her advice . . . So I went to my cousin, and told her I sought to enter the Church of England. Would she tell me what was expected of me, and teach me what it was necessary to know, before taking this step? . . . She said she would talk it over with their chaplain, and one of them would talk over any difficulties with me. My cousin was a very busy woman, so I chose the chaplain. I made my first and life-confession at my own request, and received the blessing of Absolution.

"I could see that the creeds were attempts to put into concepts something of these archetypal religious experiences which had invaded my life. I could see that the rites and ritual of the Church were means to bring folks to a living consciousness of what had been so freely given me without effort of my own. What I could not see was their insistence on the importance of Apostolic succession—or, rather, their non-recognition of ministers without such ordination.

"After four months or so, I came away unconfirmed—but that experience still pressed heavily upon me. We moved to another district, where I attended church in the nearest village. The rector there was an old dear, but I was too shy to go and talk with him. It was strengthening to read von Hugel's books, especially his two series of essays, and *St. Catherine of Genoa. He* understood all right. A friend gave me Evelyn Underhill's little book *Concerning the Inner Life.* I had previously read her *Mysticism* but was not sure if she was speaking from first-hand knowledge, because she tried to fit the Mystic experience into the framework of Vitalism. This little book was the fruit of real experience. This, and something Baron von Hugel said in his introduction to *St. Catherine of Genoa*, made me feel she would understand now. So I wrote to my friend and told her of my absolute need to be confirmed in the Church of England. She understood and helped practically about the confirmation.

"At this time I did not realise that the Church is the Body of Christ. It was the terrible impingement of the Hidden One on my consciousness and in my whole life that bowed me down in body and spirit. This direct knowledge of God drove me into His Church: this, even though I knew that many Christians appeared to be without this vivid contact. I realised before I came into it that the Church was trying to give her children what had come to me in another way.

"So after about eighteen months from the onset of that experience of the Dark Hidden One, I was confirmed. The years since have been full of adventures and discoveries, and life deeply satisfying. Thanks be to God."

In his book *Transvaluations* the poet John Redwood-Anderson[1] gives accounts of mystical experience. Through the author's kindness I have been able to read two recent poems, *Divine Appointment* and

[1] *Transvaluations* (O.U.P., Humphrey Milford, 1932)

Section XII of *Hinterland*, which form part of a new unpublished volume called *Untravelled World*. I shall attempt to present, although necessarily with extreme inadequacy, something of the tenor of these. The first poem describes two mystical experiences of early manhood, separated by about four months. Both of these seem to me properly described as moments of Illumination—of momentary and ecstatic union of soul with Spirit.[1] The mood which preceded the second of these events was one of contemplation:

> hoping nothing, despairing of nothing, uncertain and patient:
> my thoughts were as winds that have died away into silence:
> my emotions, like sheltered pools among high grasses;
> my soul, empty of pleasure and pain, empty of memory, empty of thought,
> empty of all save one bowed adoration that knelt at its wordless orison.

The poet describes how, with the onset of ecstasy, he

> stood as one crucified in the cold light of an eternal instant:
> while, from some gulf within me, some unguessed-at abyss,
> poured forth like a fountain of frozen fire, rayed out like light from its blinding core,
> a white reciprocal flight of wings to meet the wings in the sky:
> love against love—assaulting, yielding, furiously blending:
> cry and answer, voice unto voice, through the world's total silence.
> O my God, how the divine spears of your love have pierced my heart!
> how my heart, so vivified by divine death, sends upward and outward its showers of passionate arrows!
> As if two shining winds of the Spirit, one inward, one outward, careering,
> one from the infinite sphere's periphery, one from the centre's infinite depth,
> inward, and outward, spears and arrows, wing to wing flashing and answering,

[1] It is only fair to Mr. Redwood-Anderson to say that he does not accept my interpretation. He has written in a private letter of his own profound conviction "that, for the brief and timeless moment, my soul came into direct contact with God—and I mean no finite God". Another mystic to whom I put the question about being Oned with God without intermediaries replied, "It isn't that the Supreme One is undifferentiated, but that we, gathered into that Unity, lose all interest in differentiations. It is describing our attitude in beatitude: not the Divine Being." These are profound issues, and we must leave it at that.

we two in mid heaven so crashed together—crashed, and mingled,
   and passed through each other,
till my arrows had wounded your sphere's periphery, your spears
   had riddled my soul's abyss,
and we two—God and Man—were made one, yet two, in the wild
   white warfare of love.

In the course of its development the poem speaks of characteristics to which we have previously referred: the ineffable Light, the
sense of expansion and all-inclusiveness, so that all creation was felt
to be one with the poet himself.

In the second poem, *Hinterland*, there is an attempt to convey the
sense of a still deeper experience. Whereas love, as we experience it,
implies distinction and difference, the poet intuites a profounder Love
which can be realised without difference—paradoxically, a Love
which is realised in identity. He writes:

There is a knowledge beyond knowledge: a knowledge that knows
   itself not—
not itself, nor the object known, nor its own knowing;
so, too, beyond the love of person, is a love that knows not person—
not the self loving, nor the self loved, nor the love between them:
only such knowing breaks through the soul's last self-illusion;
only such love shall overcome the wound and the anguish of love:
knower and known made one in the blind state of knowledge;
lover and loved made one in the blind state of love.

When referring to the profoundest experience, Hindu thought
characteristically falls back upon negatives: "Not that, not that",
since any positive affirmation is likely to fall short of the truth. So
here the poet speaks, as, other mystics have done, of the "shining
Dark" and the "Divine Abyss"

for this, beyond time and eternity, beyond the being of God,
was to God's being what silence is to the word:
the Silence that was ere the Word was spoken,
the Word that gives shape to the Silence . . .

Writing of this poem (in a private letter) Mr. Redwood-Anderson
says:

"I have sent it for two reasons. First, for the way in which it came to
me: it came to me *as I was actually writing it*; and whether the writing
brought the experience or the experience brought the writing I am quite

unable to say. It had, in the second place, none of the wild exultation nor of the catastrophic nature of *Divine Appointment*, but was, on the contrary, very calm and infinitely mysterious. Further, on this interior journey it was as if my intellect had been 'allowed' to accompany me in a quite lowly capacity, so that it might understand what it could understand, and, where it could not, record in its own language rather than that of the emotions what was occurring spiritually . . .

"And my second reason for sending this fragment to you is that, as you will see, the experience itself goes far beyond, if I may so express it, that recorded in *Divine Appointment*. Where that was, for me, a beginning, this was rather a foretaste of the end. Where in that first experience the barrier of Difference was never passed, in this last one it *was* overpassed, *and yet without loss of identity*, and here I mean personal identity. But it is quite impossible to describe in any logical terms. If it has any analogue in ordinary earthly experience (and such an analogue can only be of the vaguest kind), it would be with the perfect *calm* that follows on a perfect consummation of erotic love: a calm in which the 'difference native to love', though still existing, ceases to be a *separation*, a calm in which both the self and the other meet in an Identity beyond the Difference, *meet but do not coalesce*."

It is inevitable that in trying to convey experience of this kind, language fails us, and our logic fails us. My own intuition (slender as it is) is that the clue to such a little understanding as we may hope for lies in an appreciation of the concept of a One-Many.

If the reader will glance again at the diagram on p. 28 we have pictured the Spirit of a Group-soul as itself a developing Being. When it becomes fully mature in Wisdom, Beauty and Love, through the myriad experiences of its souls, it joins as a perfect One-Many, the Divine Society which rules our World-System. This Divine Society, for which the term God is used in Christianity, is both transcendent to the lower evolving order and also immanent in it. It is itself a great One-Many where Group-souls constitute the "Many". It may be that it is a degree of awareness of this Divine Society which is the higher glimpse of which hints are given in this chapter. It is represented by the link (2) on the diagram. Some of the words of Case 34 may point to this, where the participant speaks of "a deeper Life than that of Spirit, mighty as that is. It was dark to the understanding. It did not cut out the Light that had been with me for the last four years. It wove into that and attracted—compelled—the attention beyond the Light. It was awesome in its hidden majesty—a Power so full and terrible in its manifoldness—something wholly *Other* than I had before been brought up against."

It is possible that there may be other still higher mystical experiences as the link (3) of the diagram is intended to convey. I doubt, however, if any human being can know anything of them: they may be possible only to perfect Group-souls.

I shall conclude this chapter, which takes us as far into the Mystery as the human mind can go—and that is a very little way—by quoting some words from my friend whose mystical experiences "on the other side" were referred to in Case 28:

Too much god = danger

"I should like to write a cautionary tale for the mystics who still occupy the confined cell of the physical body, though now and then they briefly experience what some describe as Union with God. Here is my cautionary tale:

" 'Jupiter fell in love with Semele and he revealed himself to her as a man. She thought herself strong enough to meet him on his own level, to be loved by a god. So she demanded insolently that he should come to her in his full divine status. What happened? She withered away, was consumed by his fire . . .'

"Too considerable a revelation of God would drive the most spiritual human being mad. The highly gifted mystic or yogi was never in his earthly life-time united with God. Actually, his little spark was blown on so that it became a tiny flame during the occasions he had mystical experiences. Only when the long journey through infinite time has been made, only when the human soul has been fully used for the purposes of Divine Imagination, and this soul is incomparably enriched by the strength of all the other souls in its Group can it experience Union with Divine Imagination. To be on the level with God one has to become a god, and that full glory is not to be experienced by any human being."

Chapter

7

EXPERIENCE OF THE CHRIST-SPIRIT

I could not find Him where the vestured priests
Intoned the ancient ritual of prayer.
My neighbour bowed the knee
And yet to me
He was not there.

I could not find Him where the bugles called
And men cried: "Hallelujah" to the sky.
My neighbour sobbed His name—
To her He came
And passed me by.

Yet on a busy day when spring winds blew
My billowing linen to the bleaching sun,
That Man Who served with wood
So clearly stood,
Smiling: "Well done"!

DORIS M. HOLDEN

IT may have been remarked that the accounts of mystical experience recorded in previous chapters led those who experienced them to speak of the presence of God, rather than that of Christ. This is the more remarkable since all but one had as the background of their thought and outlook the Christian ethos and Christian theology sees in Christ a mediator between God and man. What is the explanation of this?

In one or two accounts of unusual experiences which have come into my hands, persons have claimed to experience a vision of a figure whom they supposed to be the Christ. But when critical (and sympathetic) examination is made of the data, there is generally nothing to convince one that the interpretation given is valid. The experience may have been genuinely psychic and the accompanying sense of benevolence and authority in the figure may have led to this interpretation; or the experience may have been psychological, the product of causes in the subject's deeper mind. (I am assuming that we are not dealing with a disorientated mind and a delusional state.) I think most responsible persons are disposed to this viewpoint in regard to any claims implying the literal and personal appearance of Jesus Christ to a human being today.

On the other hand, there exists a considerable weight of responsible opinion which testifies to the penetrating and enduring *influence* of Jesus Christ in the hearts and minds of men today. It would be claimed that this is not an influence born just of the example and inspiration of His earthly life, but that it is something more immediate and direct than this—something therefore which is of the nature of a mystical relationship with a living and active Spirit—the Christ-Spirit. Is there any evidence to support this claim?

Let us be quite clear what we are discussing. The profound influence of Jesus Christ on the world in which we live is indubitable. It is difficult to imagine what sort of a world it would be if all that we owe to Him were removed. It is the *means* by which this influence is operative that we are considering. On what world-level does it originate?

The influence of Jesus is doubtless partly one of inspiration: His life is an example of wisdom and selfless love which has captured the admiration of successive generations. His life and teaching have been the foundation on which have arisen huge organisations—the Churches—which have maintained the significance of this teaching in the thought-life and the emotional life of mankind ever since. This organisational aspect plays a very large part in preserving the influence of Jesus Christ in the life of today. The mystical factor is to outward appearance a small one—but nevertheless, I believe, an absolutely vital one. If it were not present, nothing is more certain than that these organisations, cut off from this vital source, would slowly perish—and perish utterly (as most other organisations do after a time of fashion or usefulness). You cannot maintain indefinitely a living religion which has power in the hearts and lives of men by a process of suggestion (and, where this fails, by threats), however well organised. This, I think, is why, in *The Cloud of Unknowing* it is said that the safety of any state depends on the number of contemplatives who reside within it.

I shall present here two accounts, which I do not regard as fully mystical in the sense in which the term has been used in this book (of this I am not sure), but which point to the activity of the Christ-Spirit as their source, radiating into the higher mental levels of the world. The first of these is from the lady of Case 34.

Case 35 (X. Y.)

"The Jesus of History was a great leader—Dominus—Lord. Yes, but God is all-mighty and creative beyond our span of thought. I just couldn't see for years how God could become incarnate in a man: it seemed nonsense.

"Then a book by one of the most advanced of what are called the 'Higher Critics' was lent to me. It set out to show in devastating thoroughness that the Christ of the 'Gospel according to St. John' was a fabrication of men's mind, without any personal historic existence. It was a clever book, and I read to the end with increasing interest. I put the book down on the table before me. I can see the last page in my mind's eye still. Still more realistically I recall what happened to me then. I was suffused with the spirit of the Living Christ. I knew then what the author of that gospel meant when he wrote. 'We beheld His glory, the glory of the only-begotten Son of God: full of Grace and Truth.'

"An intuition of the mighty *Truth* held me above images and thought: something beyond anything my mind had sought. It was only later when I came down to lower levels of apprehension that my thoughts tried to crystallise something of what I had lived through. My thoughts laughed to themselves: 'Well, even if you did not know before, as you do now, that Jesus lived and *is* alive, your own native gumption should have told you it would be even more wonderful if a group of men in the early Church had made up this picture of the divine Christ.' If they had made it up there would be patterns of 'divine sonship' in each of them. And so there are indeed—buds called into living expression by the innate divinity of the man Jesus.

"And behind all these patterns must be some archetypal pattern of sonship, which *must* manifest: if not then, then at some point in time. And now I could see the Divine event cutting into time."

This experience clearly brought to the mind of the percipient an Illumination of complete authority.

The account which follows is a précis and a few extracts from an unpublished autobiography. It describes how a human soul which had touched perhaps the lowest point of desolation and anguish—and had crossed that fine line which separates sanity from insanity—found within itself, planted quite inexplicably, "a tiny seed" of peace and conviction.

Case 36

The writer is a woman in middle life who bears a name distinguished for two generations in English scholarship and politics. The background of childhood was thoroughly happy.

"All that makes life perfectly delicious: colours, flowers, warmth, food—all that children love in activity: swimming, riding, climbing, inventing games or creating things with hands, all these were ours to the full. We were ever spurred on and animated by adults who were always full of invention and good spirits. To add to this, our parents were very much in love. We took it as the norm to have a father and mother, both very beautiful and healthy and happy who loved each other and us."

Her parents' attitude to religious things was quietly agnostic, but the child herself appeared to have an intuitive awareness of the existence of God.

"I could feel a sort of cloud around my head which made me know God was. This is such a silly way to explain it, yet it is the most finite form I know. It was as though God, having perhaps His Being, concentrated afar, yet radiated out this Being from Himself to each of His creation, and had given them as sort of spiritual feelers this cloud which enabled them to know He was. For me, this perception was so clear that I couldn't make out why my parents had not got it also . . . Life was secure because of this luminous cloud and because of the love of my parents; it was a pleasure to be alone because of this cloud, and increasingly difficult to be for very long with people, because they ate up the cloud so that one was left dry, remote and unprotected. Some people ate up the cloud quicker than others. By the time I was seven I constantly wished I could be put in prison, because that was the only way I could conceive of being alone for long stretches."

In the light of adult experience it is worth noting that religious convictions which were later born out of intense suffering owe little to ideas planted by parents or others in the child's mind. The years which led up to the main experience will be summarised briefly. There was the beauty and freshness of youthful love, the sudden and unexpected death of the beloved, and two very unusual dream experiences relating to him. There was a year at Oxford leading to the conviction that this was not the right path. There was a three-and-a-half months' trek across Canada with a rucksack and a tent.

"Being twenty-one, I started to find myself . . . I wanted to find more than myself: I wanted to find out what the whole set-up was about—why we were born, where we were going, who God was, and why. Nothing less than a cross between a battering-ram and a key combined would keep me quiet. So my feet took me on and on every day, and the nights stretched out above me with endless stars. I had enough time to think at last, and think as *I* thought, not as all the great writers of the world thought. For books are most strange things: they are food but they are not keys. I had read of the great religions of the East and West, and lived in the imagination of poets, but when I lifted my head from a book to look for a moment out of a window, my heart always said, 'You'll never find truth in the printed page. When all books have gone up in flames, Truth—Life itself—will still abide'."

At twenty-three years of age this lady married a German aged thirty-six, and went to live with him in a small musical college of which he was the Director, in an East German town. At the time of the birth of her first daughter came also the rise of Hitler into power, and with this the tragedy of the Nazi regime. Her husband was immature psychologically, and offered her no security or understanding. An ideological gulf grew up and yawned between them. Three weeks after the birth of her second daughter the strains proved too great to be borne, and she passed for six weeks into the "no-man's land of madness". Emotionally isolated, cut off from all that the English tradition stood for, psychically sensitive to the destructive emotions moving in the German Unconscious, she says:

"A great sadness without seeming cause or reason descended on me—a sadness too great for tears or words . . . I was in no understandable bodily anguish: this was a dark pressure of numbness, which was growing every moment, and of which I had never heard."

Memory started to fail. Insomnia followed, and through the interminable hours of darkness there followed a desperate struggle to hold on to sanity. Weeks of utter blackness and despair followed, with the sense of forces "leading me nearer and nearer to a door which was far too small for me. It wasn't my physical body which would get squashed, it was *me*, my actual self." Yet amid the blackness and delusional states there was retained a central point of insight.

"If I, born into the world with such a sure knowledge that God is, could have, in less than thirty years, landed myself into such darkness, how must it be for those others who are born, for some reason, without this all-consuming knowledge of God's Being? In the country in which I then lived, I could feel a panting unrest, like a lion padding up and down behind the cage-bars, because the peaceful freedom of God was not known. Everywhere that I looked in that night I saw the same great abyss, caused by sin and worldliness, fixed between the heavenly Realms and all of us on earth; and there was no bridge across the darkness."

During one night of anguish there came a sudden impulse to look at an old Bible.

"You know how it says in books, 'scales fell from my eyes'; I have always thought it such a silly phrase. But at that moment that is what happened to me in very truth . . . *The bridge from Heaven to Earth, from Earth to Heaven, was accomplished for all time. Christ Himself was the bridge from Heaven to Earth, from Earth to Heaven . . .*

"And now within me, in I believe my heart, something happened. Instead of the chaos and the sorrow there was a tiny seed planted. It was so small and frail that I felt that I should keep my hands round it to protect it. It was a seed of utter peace, not of stillness and negation, but potent with creation. I didn't plant it, nor was it me; it was something new and full of endless possibilities. Could it be extinguished or torn up by outer opposition? Could it be stifled by my own action or neglect? That I didn't know. I felt sure and quiet in my knowledge of it. It was the greatest gift one could receive on earth and it had lodged in me, at my weakest, my darkest, my maddest moment. I sat on the edge of the bed and knew that I need neither hurry nor fight nor mourn for as long as I lived. CHRIST WAS. He didn't need me or you or anybody, but He could use us; indeed He could live in us. I looked at the world again and saw it differently . . . I knew myself to be well, but still very weak and easily knocked off my Rock of Peace . . . It became, in the months that followed, one of the hardest things to bear, that what to me were eternal truths were for others but the signs of madness . . .

"How the baby and I spent the rest of the night is hard to explain, for though she lay in her cot and I lay in my bed beside her, we didn't seem to be on earth at all. I prayed without any words, lying, as it were, with my heart against God's, often just resting, but sometimes with returning terrors. It seemed that I was quite naked out of eternity, floating with the child outside space and time. There was nothing to cover or protect us. There was nothing of earthly comfort or security to hold us. I saw conceptions like the motet '*Furchte Dich Nicht*' which we had just been singing a month before, as having an eternal shape—as having always been there, and Bach but embodying it, bringing it to earth. I found that music was the purest of links between people, far surpassing in clarity our words or deeds, which were always smudged by personality. This first came to me as a truth, into my thinking, but later in the night as the babe and I sailed around between heaven and earth, I heard a singing sound of a myriad stars. The wonder of it was both in the quality of the sound and the fact that every possible tone was singing forth at the same time yet without making any discord. As I listened, I started to remember my own existence and so moved back again into my body. With an effort, I thought, 'I am hearing the music of the spheres', and therefore tried to move away from myself. For a moment or two I succeeded and listened with spiritual ears to a sound never consciously heard before by me—then I slipped right into my body (too soon, alas) where my physical ears could hear nothing but the ticking of the clock and the far whistle of a train over the frozen snow. Till then I had half-thought the music of the spheres was a poetical fancy. Now I got the distinct impression that the sound was caused by the movement in the heavens, and also that all music composed on earth was the result of people hearing this heavenly music within themselves, even if not consciously. Since that time I have heard the music only once again. When in England a few months later, returning from sleep I found myself looking down from the foot of my bed at my body lying on the bed. At that moment I was aware of a great sense of peace, and almost heavenly quality, and then I heard again the music of the spheres for a moment before I stepped once again into my body and opened my eyes again to a new day."

From this night of crisis there was no looking back. Sustained by faith in the power of the "Christ-seed", she slowly found her way back to health and normality. A number of psychical experiences took place in the period of convalescence. One of these was the strange sight of a brigade of German soldiers passing through the town; but she saw them all as marching corpses. Her interpretation was that either it meant that they had all been killed in their personalities, or it meant that they would all be dead within a few years. There were several symbolical visions of the gathering evil in Germany. There was also a sensitivity to the forces of good at work in the world. She says:

"When I could read very little because of weakness, and when many of the human contacts were negative, I found myself upheld in a new and inner way by people living on earth whom I could not see. Where we were living, the influences of East and West seemed to cross one another and meet and mingle. Through many days and nights, until I returned to what might be called a fairly normal existence, it seemed that there were people living in the East, possibly in Tibet, possibly in India, who had a vision and insight into spiritual things that we in the West completely lacked. I was aware at night of a group of people, men I think, who were living together somewhere east of me, who were of such spiritual stature and insight that they could perceive the conflict that was going on in a small town in East Germany. I felt myself seen and supported by them in my struggles and uncertainties. If one knows one is watched, one's conduct is apt to be strengthened; mine certainly was, by realising that they could see at that distance. At times I came to feel, 'Without them I could not have got through and I felt for them great thankfulness, and often I hoped that they knew and accepted my thanks. And being helped and supported so from the East, I saw our western Bible in quite a new light. It was as though there was a vast spiritual world from which our

Bible with its great truths had been gleaned, but this world was infinitely larger than could be revealed to one race or in one book. Nothing less than a World Bible would suffice, a gathering together of even a modicum of the spiritual truths throughout all time. I remembered all I had read from the writings of India. They seemed to be in no conflict with Christianity. They looked to the same source, spoke of the same God and Creator: it was only that Christ had made the final and continuous bridge . . . Here was a gift from the Godhead bridging the gulf for aye, not just one of us looking upward towards the Father."

It is perhaps only necessary to add that, twenty years later, this woman is giving herself in happy and selfless service in the name of Christ to her fellowmen.

The central part of this life-drama is the experience, "There was a tiny seed planted . . . It was a seed of utter peace, not of stillness and negation but potent with creation." This seed of knowledge, as in the previous case, was a word of complete authority. It was sown in an extremity of need, and worked a psychological miracle.

Such events as these are, I suggest, evidence of the activity of the Christ-Spirit. In both cases it was an Illumination of the levels of mind and not an immediate relation with the Christ-Spirit Himself. With considerable diffidence I shall suggest an answer to the question raised at the beginning of the chapter. I believe that Jesus was a member of the Divine Society before His incarnation in Palestine, and that He resumed this relationship after His resurrection. He is therefore a member of the One-Many whom men call "God", and mystical experience which implies an immediate relationship with Christ involves the comparatively rare higher step marked (2) on p. 28. This does not mean that His love is any less accessible or His influence further removed.[1] It should mean, however, that a great deal more humility and reverence are proper to our lowly state. We talk too lightly of the sublimities. A momentary union with the Christ-Spirit would be an experience for which few indeed can be ready, something for which language is inadequate (as we saw in the previous chapter). It must be remembered that we are not discussing the Jesus of history, whose personality made its impact two thousand years ago on men and women like ourselves. We are discussing a powerful Spirit, one of the Divine Hierarchy which men call God, whose influence is now untempered (as it was in Palestine) by the limitation of a human personality.

[1] I think there are profundities of meaning in St. John xvi, very much beyond those involved in the customary exegesis.

In a remarkable little book called *The Golden Fountain*[1] a modern mystic gives accounts of a number of experiences of deepening penetration. After what the subject called her first "conversion", the historic figure of Jesus continued to be the focus of her love and devotion. Of later mystical experience she says:

"It produced a fundamental alteration of my whole outlook and grasp on life. It brought me into direct contact with God, and was the commencement of a total change of heart and mind and consciousness; the centre of my consciousness, without any effort of my own, suddenly moving bodily from a concentration upon the visible or earthly, to a loving and absorbed concentration upon, and a fixed attention to, the Invisible God—a most amazing, undreamed-of change, which remained permanent, though fluctuating through innumerable degrees of intensity before coming to a state of equilibrium. And so Christ went away from me, so that I adored Him in God."

I think it is probable that this is higher mystical experience such as Case 34 presented.

[1] Published by John M. Watkins, London, 1st Ed., 1919, 2nd Ed., 1936

Chapter

8

THE EVALUATION OF MYSTICAL EXPERIENCE

Clasp thou of Truth the central core!
Hold fast that centre's central sense!
An atom there shall fill thee more
Than realms on Truth's circumference.

AUBREY T. DE VERE

Up to this point we have considered accounts of mystical experience
as it has come to ordinary people in many walks of life. We have also
suggested a conceptual framework within which the data may be
classified. It is now proposed to summarise the generally held views
as to the steps on the way of classical mysticism, so that we may look
at our own data in the light of these views.

CLASSICAL MYSTICISM: STEPS OF THE WAY

All through the centuries there have been a few men and women,
not confined to any particular race or religious tradition, whose lives
were completely devoted to the supreme quest of the soul. The study
of their lives and writings has led to the recognition of several stages
or phases of the mystic way. They are not clearly distinguishable but
tend to merge into each other. We follow Evelyn Underhill,[1] one of
the authorities in this field, in the account given below.

(1) *The Awakening of the Self*. Here the soul becomes intensely
aware that there is a Divine Reality to be known and that the pursuit
of this is more worthwhile than anything else. The majority of people
are not awake in this sense. The sensory world dominates their thought,
their desires and their action. The awakened self knows that the sensory
world will never satisfy it, and knows also the way it *must* take.

(2) *Purgation or Purification*. This is the long and arduous path
of self-discipline and self-denial; the perfection of character by the
elimination of all that is centred on self. It has often taken the form
of severe ascetic practices combined with the continuous life of prayer
or "orison". The traditional disciplines which have marked this path
have been poverty, chastity and obedience. They have been described
as three forms of poverty: of possession, of the senses, and of the
will. The idea behind them is self-naughting, so that the sense of

---

[1] Evelyn Underhill, *Mysticism* (Methuen & Co. Ltd., 1949 Ed.)

X being a separate self with desires and rights is replaced by the sense of being a servant of the Divine Will.)It is not the outward act which primarily matters but the attitude of inner renunciation of every-thing which would hinder the soul on its way to God. It is said that the Curé d'Ars would not permit himself the pleasure of smelling a rose, lest it should draw him away from the single goal of his life. Although we may ourselves feel more in sympathy with St. Francis, who ordered that a garden of flowers should be planted in a convent "in order that all who saw them might remember the Eternal Sweetness", we cannot but admire from afar the utter devotion which is prepared to sacrifice itself completely rather than be distracted on the way to God.

(3) *Illumination*. This is described by Evelyn Underhill as "the great swing back into sunshine which is the reward of that painful descent into the 'cell of self-knowledge' ".[1] "A lifting of conscious-ness from a self-centred to a God-centred world is of the essence of illumination."[2] It is clear that in this stage the mystic has permanent access to a level of consciousness far above that of ordinary men. The descriptions of Illumination which mystics give to us are of great variety, and are doubtless influenced by the temperament of the subject. There are two contrasting types, although many a mystic may find himself able to use the language of both. They correspond respectively to those who apprehend Reality in transcendental and in immanent terms. The first are awe-struck in the presence of the Infinite, where mystery upon mystery is disclosed to the apprehend-ing soul. The second use the language of the heart, and for them Love is the key to the universe. Thus, a mystic of the latter type speaks of the "rippling tide of love which flows secretly from God into the soul and draws it mightily back into its source".

Illumination is a supremely blissful state, one of clear and con-scious awareness of the presence of God. The self is said to "meet God in the ground of the soul". Along with this, inevitably goes a new level of perception of the world around, which appears everywhere as sacramental. It has been described by Evelyn Underhill as "the discovery of the Perfect One self-revealed in the Many, not the forsaking of the Many to find the One". Those who have experienced the wonder and thrill of this have tried to find words to express it. Erigena said, "Every visible and invisible creature is a theophany or appearance of God." Dean Inge was prepared to define mysticism as "the attempt to realise the presence of the living God in the soul

---

[1] *loc. cit.*, p. 233   [2] *loc. cit.*, p. 234

and in nature", or more generally as "the attempt to realise, in thought and feeling, the immanence of the temporal in the eternal and of the eternal in the temporal".

Browning wrote of such an experience:

> I but open my eyes—and perfection, no more and no less,
> In the kind I imagined full-fronts me, and God is seen God
> In the star, in the stone, in the flesh, in the soul and the clod.

"The sense of the divine presence", says Evelyn Underhill, "may go side by side with the daily life and normal mental activities of its possessor, who is not necessarily an ecstatic or an abstracted visionary remote from the work of the world."[1] In the phase of Illumination there is no loss of the sense of individuality. "His heightened apprehension of Reality lights up rather than obliterates the rest of his life: and may even increase his power of dealing adequately with the accidents of normal existence."[2] Finally, one of the common aspects of the Illuminated state is the awareness of a radiant and ineffable light. Miss Underhill expresses the view that this general testimony is not metaphorical, but is an attempt to convey an actual experience.

(4) *The Dark Night of the Soul.* Western mystics, who have reached the stage of Illumination and seek to go further, often pass through a stage (which may last for months or years) which is described as a Dark Night. "Those who go on," says Evelyn Underhill, "are the great and strong spirits who do not seek to *know* but are drawn to *be.*"[3] They find themselves not merely blocked on the way forward, but apparently thrown back into darkness and cast out from the presence of God. Their power of orison or contemplation leaves them, and sometimes outer circumstances seem to be in league with the inner mood of adversity, to subject the soul to a desperate final testing of its nature. Speaking of this dark night of the soul Evelyn Underhill says:

"In some temperaments it is the emotional aspect—the anguish of the lover who has suddenly lost the Beloved—which predominates: in others the intellectual darkness and confusion overwhelms everything else. Some have felt it, with St. John of the Cross, as a passive purification, a state of helpless misery, in which the self does nothing, but lets Life have its way with her. Others, with Suso and the virile mystics of the German school, have experienced it rather as a period of strenuous activity and moral conflict directed to that total self-abandonment which is the

[1] *loc. cit.*, p. 243   [2] *loc. cit.*, p. 246   [3] *loc. cit.*, p. 383

essential preparation of the unitive life. Those elements of character which were unaffected by the first purification of the self—left as it were in a corner when the consciousness moved to the level of the illuminative life—are here roused from their sleep, purged of illusion, and forced to join the growing stream."[1]

It is also said that this phase is "to cure the soul of the innate tendency to seek and rest in spiritual joys; to confuse Reality with the joy given by the contemplation of Reality."[2] "In the Dark Night the starved and tortured spirit learns through an anguish, which is itself an orison, to accept lovelessness for the sake of Love, nothingness for the sake of the All; dies without any sure promise of life, loses when it hardly hopes to find."[3]

It is an agonising phase through which many of the great Western mystics appear to have passed. Their emergence from it has been through a complete surrender of the finite self: the willingness to abandon even individuality (although it is given back again). It is a phase of tearing loose from the last links of the world of Becoming to gain a conscious foothold in the One-Many of the world of Being. Perhaps we should rather say that, with these fetters severed, Becoming and Being are wholly reconciled for them.

(5) *The Unitive Life.* This is the goal of the mystic's quest. In Illumination the mystic is aware of the presence of God. But in the Unitive Life he is in union with Him, and permanently establishes a centre of consciousness in this relationship. Mystics of the transcendent-metaphysical type speak of this as "deification"; mystics of the immanent-personal type refer to "the spiritual marriage". Both phrases attempt to convey a sense of permanent union of God with the soul, but none of the Western mystics give any support to a complete loss of individuality. St. Augustine says, "My life shall be a real life, being wholly full of Thee."

Evelyn Underhill gives three marks of the Unitive Life:[4]

(a) A complete absorption in the interests of the Infinite under whatsoever mode It is apprehended by the self.

(b) A consciousness of sharing Its strength, acting by Its authority, which results in a complete sense of freedom, an invulnerable serenity, and usually urges the self to some form of heroic effort or creative activity.

(c) The establishment of the self as a "power for life", a centre of energy, an actual parent of spiritual vitality in other men.

[1] *loc. cit.*, p. 388   [2] *loc. cit.*, p. 395
[3] *loc. cit.*, p. 397   [4] *loc. cit.*, p. 416

"These rare personalities in whom it is found", says Miss Under-hill, "are the media through which that Triumphing Spiritual Life, which is the essence of Reality, forces an entrance into the temporal order and begets children.[1]

In every generation, and in all religions, there have been souls here and there who have attained to the stage of Illumination: a few very rare souls are perhaps living the Unitive Life. Of these latter all we may say is that their presence on Earth is not a necessity as far as they are concerned. They are here of their own free will to help needy humanity, although for the most part their high attainment is quite unknown to mankind.

Before leaving this summary of the stages of classical mysticism I should like to make a few remarks on "the dark night of the soul". As previously stated, this description is properly used of mystics who have reached Illumination and strive to go further. There is, however, at a much lower level of spiritual attainment, an experience which comes to many ordinary people and which merits this description. Perhaps they have been raised to a point of ecstasy and dedication through some moving preacher's influence. They may have had glimpses of near-Illuminative levels, but after the rapture a reaction sets in, and they surge back into self-dissatisfaction, despair, frustration and the darkest of nights. They need the help of someone who combines psycho-therapeutic skill with religious understanding—and such persons are rare. If any of my readers are passing through such a "dark night", it may help them to know that the cause of their state is that the soul's growth has not been gradual enough. They had a glimpse of the Delectable Mountains, and assumed that they had almost arrived. Spiritual distances can be deceptive, and disappointment can be correspondingly great. If they cannot find a competent adviser in their need, they need not continue in despair. The glimpse which was intended to be an inspiration was mistaken for an achievement, and the way through is to face the mistake, and take up courageously the pilgrim's way, knowing that the goal is there and will some day be attained.

ASSESSMENTS AND COMPARISONS

We have now reached a stage where we can evaluate the accounts given in earlier chapters in the light of the classical stages of the mystic way. There can be little doubt that it is the characteristics

[1] *loc. cit.*, p. 432

of the third stage called Illumination which are found in the best of the spontaneous accounts. In most cases, this state was touched and held for a short time. Sometimes the terms describing the experience were ecstatic, but the state itself was not permanent. It came spontaneously, it could not be sustained indefinitely, nor could it be re-entered at will. Only in this respect does it appear to differ from the classical type of experience which, in its full development, creates a permanent centre on this level of consciousness. Only the person of Case 34 appeared to have a natural aptitude for a permanent or very prolonged Illuminative state. By "natural aptitude" I refer of course to the soul's quality, and not to any physically inherited capacity. I believe that a soul can only experience what it has qualified itself to experience, whether in previous lives or the current one. There is no evidence of any way to a state of permanent Illumination or God-awareness other than that long road of purification of character and aspiration which has been followed by mystics of both East and West. One who spoke with authority, long ago, said, "Blessed are the pure in heart: for they shall see God."

The sense of the Divine Presence or "meeting God in the ground of the soul" which is characteristic of Illumination is certainly an awareness of God immanent, but it is (in our view) God immanent in the Spirit of the Group-soul, and it is with this Spirit that the soul's union is at this stage established. The Unitive Life is then interpreted as achieving step (2) on p. 28 so that a permanent level of consciousness is attained within the Divine Society which men call God. Any member of this One-Many may truly say, "I and my Father are One", or may say, "The Son can do nothing but what he sees the Father doing." The Many act as One; the One acts as Many. The Many know and feel as One; the One knows and feels as Many. We are now in the realm of paradox if we attempt to say anything. Even for this inconceivably great Divine Society which rules our galaxy on all its levels, the Supreme One—Divine Imagining—(the Fount and Origin of All, yet Unmanifest)—is immanent in It, but must also transcend It.

MYSTICISM AND RELIGION

The reader who is reasonably familiar with the language and the ideas of religion but not familiar with the more metaphysical ideas which spring from mystical experience may find it hard to reconcile the two. I shall therefore try at this point to make their relationship clear.

At its heart, religion is mystical, in that it has to do with each soul's relationship to a higher spiritual order. The great religions of the world have generally collected the teachings of some spiritually advanced soul whose experience of this higher order has been intimate and at first-hand. The founders of the great religions have been mystics. Now teachings are attempts to convey in language to others high experiences and insights in the realm of Spirit. In a process where the mind is inevitably used to give them expression, all the limitations of language and logic are imposed upon them. For this reason, as far as possible, the highest truths of religion are conveyed through symbolism, myth and parable. When Reality lies beyond words it can only be suggested by these indirect means. How often in the New Testament we are told, "The Kingdom of Heaven is like . . ." and even then the phrase "Kingdom of Heaven" is suggestive and analogical only. *There is no perfect way of conveying to others what can only be known by experience.* We must therefore recognise the inherent limitations of creeds and belief-systems which all religions preserve and revere. They are certainly of great value, just as maps, signposts and guide-books are of value to the traveller. Unfortunately, undue emphasis has all too frequently been placed upon a knowledge of these aids instead of upon familiarity with the country to which they refer. Moreover, although the map-makers have never agreed among themselves, independent explorers have always been viewed with some concern, if not suspicion.

What we desire to make clear is that "religion" has three aspects: a mythical core, an intellectual formulation, and, finally, certain ritual practices. These last serve to unite the faithful, and permit many people to share in a fellowship and find mutual encouragement in a way of life which the beliefs enjoin. These practices often include elements of a magical nature, originally designed to produce, or assist in producing, changes in consciousness. The inwardness of these is little recognised today. With regard to the intellectual formulations, we are not here concerned with their differences, but only with the limitation which they all share in common because Mind has constructed them.

The language of religion speaks of God as an *object* of worship, while we are the worshipping subjects. He is therefore regarded as a Being apart from other beings, even though supreme attributes are ascribed to Him. In other words, God is transcendent—wholly other than ourselves. This implies that as finite beings we are a limitation upon his infinity; our wills are a limitation upon His will, even though as a poet has said, "Our wills are ours to make them Thine." It is this gulf between man and a transcendent God which Christian theology bridges by the God-Man or Saviour, Jesus Christ. There remain, of course, unresolved problems so far as the Nature of Jesus Christ is concerned, and these have been the subject matter of much theological controversy.

In the language of religion, God created, by His fiat, the Heavens and the Earth. He created them "from nought", by which it is meant to convey that creation is not to be regarded as of God's "substance", but rather as the type of creation which operates when a poem is created in a poet's mind. It is broadly true to say that no religion could hope or expect to meet the intimate emotional needs of mankind which could not offer more than the belief in God transcendent, or wholly "other". Long before the birth of Christ, the insight of great souls had recognised that the relationship of God and man was a great deal more than merely this. I may cite the Hebrew psalmist as one of those who recognised that there was a relationship of love and interest involved.

"Like as a father pitieth his children, So the Lord pitieth them that fear Him. For He knoweth our frame; He remembereth that we are dust." When St. Paul addressed the Athenians, "In Him we live and move and have our being; as certain even of your own poets have said, 'For we are also His offspring'," he was proclaiming in unmistakable terms the immanence of God in His Creation. It is a part of orthodox religious belief that we should hold to both the transcendence and the immanence of God, even though no logical reconciliation is possible. This is the price we pay for attempting to express in language experience which has its reality on a level beyond that of Mind.[1]

Let us turn now to the mystical descriptions of Reality. These emphasise, firstly, the one-ness of the whole—barriers dividing subject and object disappear. Secondly, time seems to exist no longer in the familiar sense. Thirdly, the emotional tones of Reality are utterly satisfying—they are harmonious, blissful and perfect—the quintessence of Love irradiates the whole. When the mystics endeavour to account for their experience, the term "God" alone seems adequate. It is clear that mystical experience finds its explanation in terms of the immanence of God.

[1] It may be pointed out that physicists face a similar situation, holding to classical and quantum ideas simultaneously. It is the price to be paid for holding on to familiar ideas of space, time and matter, in a region where they do not strictly apply.

Observe, however, how marked is the contrast between the ordinary man's outlook and the mystic's. For the ordinary man the world is one of ten thousand things: for the mystic it is a great Unity of which he is a part. For the plain man God is remote and unseen: for the mystic the world is full of God. With regard to Time, the plain man would say with Andrew Marvell:

> But at my back I always hear
> Time's wingèd chariot hurrying near

while the mystic feels he is somehow above time. The ordinary man, looking at the world, is aware of conflict, unrest, tragedy, accident, suffering and sorrow; the mystic speaks of harmony, peace, love, perfection and pattern. The plain man lives in a universe which includes the One *and* the Many. As an element of the latter he worships, loves and prays to the One. The mystic finds himself a part of a great Unity, and describes Reality as a One-Many in which he participates. How can these strangely contrasting views be reconciled? Not by claiming that one view is true and the other is false, but by recognising that both are true from their respective standpoints. Their standpoints are, however, very different.

Perhaps we may illustrate the difference between them by considering the quality of perfection in relation to the diagram on p. 28. Across the middle of the diagram a line has been drawn. Let us take the standpoint of the ordinary man who is one of the Many. Above this line is the perfect One (The Divine Society) which men call God. Below the line are the imperfect Many, still evolving (or involving). But now, let us move our standpoint to that of the Divine Society. It does not know itself as a One above with a Many below. It knows itself as a One-Many still imperfect, for an aspect of itself is still evolving. In its Unity every sentient creature has a part. The Divine Society is "bringing many sons unto glory" in the process of Becoming.

The Divine Society incorporates the archetypal pattern for *our* world-system (i.e. our galaxy, on all its levels of reality). In the great process of realising this plan, myriads of Group-souls each take charge of a small part of it, and are in many cases properly described as sub-imaginal fields for the working out of the implications of this part. On lower levels of the world-system, those which Plotinus called the "sensible world", and which we have called Mind, the plan is expressed and precipitated. By their participation in this vast experiment souls come to fully-conscious knowledge of belonging to a higher Unity, and through their experience Group-souls grow towards the "perfection" of the Divine Society. This hierarchical conception of the One-Many is all inclusive. One life flows through the whole, just as the life of a great tree flows through the trunk into all the branches, twigs and leaves. If a self-conscious leaf could be imagined looking out at other leaves, having no knowledge of the branches, trunk and roots, or of the life flowing through the whole structure, we have a parallel to our position as creatures in the physical world. It is a world of separateness and individuality which our minds try to interpret and understand. The language and concepts of religion apply to this world-level.

On the other hand, suppose the roots and trunk were self-conscious and aware of the life flowing through them, the tree would know itself to be a unity finding expression and growth through a multiplicity of aspects—branches, twigs, leaves, etc. Here we have a parable of God immanent—the great One-Many. Let us realise what it implies. Not a sparrow falls to the ground without the Whole suffering loss. When I love or hate, when I do good or do evil, when I rejoice and when I sorrow, it is not I alone that do these things: the One also experiences them. On this outlook sin is the denial by man of his relationship with the Whole, and his consequent acting as though he alone mattered. In simple terms all sin is self-centredness (when there is the capacity to be otherwise).

J. Redwood-Anderson[1] has expressed this clearly:

"The trouble begins when man asserts his peripheral position to be central: this is Original Sin. All asceticism is designed to break the mortal hold of the egocentric and anthropocentric obsession. One should not abandon the world, one should embrace the world; but this is safe and right only when one has abandoned oneself. It is not attachment to an object of desire, whatever that object may be, that is a barrier to the spiritual life, but attachment to oneself *in that attachment* . . . If we could remember that all our experiences are not only ours—not our exclusive private property and concern—but also and identically God's; if we could remember that we are not only ends in ourselves, but also means to the total end: not only self-active organisms (I speak spiritually), but also organs in the Divine Organism—if we could remember this single and simple fact, we should be very near to the mystical life . . . We should do nothing we were ashamed of, since in our shame God is also ashamed; we should not wittingly do anything to another's hurt, since in that hurt—

[1] From an article entitled "The Fourth Mysticism" published in *Faith and Freedom* (Spring and Summer issues, 1951. A Unitarian Journal published at Manchester College, Oxford).

God is also hurt—and in the hurt thereby done to ourselves God is again hurt. We should be living then *as if* we lived 'within' and not 'without'.''

By living "within" and "without" Redwood-Anderson refers to two contrasting viewpoints. The first is the view from the centre, as the One sees it, and as the individual soul sees it also in mystical experience. The second is the view from the periphery as the ordinary man sees it. The first view is harmonious, unified, purposeful and significant, the life of a growing organism. The second view is full of conflict and oppositions and seems to have neither meaning nor pattern in it. Indeed, to many people searching wistfully for a philosophy of life, it is this very appearance of life as a meaningless sequence of chance happenings which is the most oppressive problem. After pointing out that from the "outward" standpoint "ninety-nine hundredths of our customary significant experiences are set in a chaotic sea of non-significance", Redwood-Anderson says:

"Could we see from all time and simultaneously all the events of the Universe—see them from inside as well as from outside—nothing could appear as irrelevant to the whole pattern: there would be no non-significant matrix, but a single all-comprehending significance, and that in turn means a single all-comprehending truth and beauty and rightness. This is the characteristic of the Divine Experience; and this can in its measure be known and shared by the soul that has abandoned its peripheral isolation . . . and taken up a central position.

"Man must live his life as man, a finite being here on this earth, with his individual and finite values, his individual desires, his loves and his hates, his joys and his sorrows: and, *at the same time*, man must live that life and realise it as a function of the organic life of the Whole—an autonomous organ of the Divine Experience. This is, I believe, the whole secret of how to experience rightly—a secret nobody ever tells us.''

I do not think this truth could have been expressed more clearly. When we look at a system of relationships such as the diagram on p. 28 attempts to convey, there are always two viewpoints, no matter what one's location on the diagram may be. A soul on the periphery may look inward at the Spirit, to which it draws near in Illumination, and say, "I have attained to God." The Spirit from its centre may look outward and say, "My child, you are where you have always been—but now you know it." Becoming and Being are the inward-looking and the outward-looking views. St. Paul was both mystic and man of action, and he expressed this truth when he said, "Work out your own salvation . . . for it is God that worketh in you.''

MYSTICISM AND OCCULTISM

The saint and the sage are types of advanced achievement on different, though not incompatible, paths. The one has striven to be selfless and the other to be wise. Mystic and occultist are specialised types of the saint and the sage, putting the emphasis respectively on being and knowing. The mystic's one desire is God, and his path is generally that of love and devotion—a way which Hindu thought calls Bhakti Yoga. The occultist seeks to understand the created universe on all its levels of significance, and Hindu thought calls this Jnana Yoga.

We shall not attempt to define mysticism, believing that if an intuitive apprehension of it is not possible, words add nothing of value. Evelyn Underhill once spoke of it as the "art of union with Reality", and this conveys the truth without defining it.

Occultism is a term which connotes very different things to different people. Popularly it is regarded as the sum of all those systems of teaching and practice which are described by their exponents as possessing secret knowledge about non-physical levels of the world. It is a most curious collection of interwoven knowledge and superstition, suggesting a variety of jig-saw puzzles from which many important key-fragments are missing. The term would embrace the Mysteries of Ancient Greece and Egypt of which little is known except that they were esteemed by some revered figures of the Ancient World. It would include Gnosticism, Tantric Yoga, Masonry, Alchemy, Astrology, systems of divination such as the I Ching, Cabbalistic teaching, Rosicrucian teaching, Theosophy, Anthroposophy, the teaching of Gurdjieff-Ouspensky, etc. All have their devotees, and I do not propose to comment on any of them, since by occultism in the context of this book I mean only the way of knowledge—more particularly, knowledge of the supra-sensory levels of the world. Pursued in the spirit of a love of truth, occultism has the same claim to consideration as scientific enquiry on the physical level. It might be described—a little fancifully perhaps—as "thinking God's thoughts after Him", but at least it is an intrinsically worthy pursuit. There is no reason why men should not desire to know as much about the powers of mind as they have learned about the physical world.

All this is reasonable, as long as we do not forget that there are always dangers involved in the extension of knowledge. Unless the man who augments his knowledge possesses also purity of motive and character, it is obvious that this only makes him a more powerful man—not a humbler, nobler and wiser man. The way of Knowledge, where it is unrelated to a deep humility, almost inevitably tends to strengthen the walls of self, and where this happens its results are in complete contrast with mystical achievement which dissolves the walls of self. Because this is so often the case it falls under Miss Underhill's rather sweeping disparagement. She identifies occultism with a very limited aspect of it—magic—which is the manipulation of events of the physical world through using the paranormal powers of mind. Its self-seeking and self-aggrandising character is the basis of her distrust and condemnation. She says, "It is an individualistic and acquisitive science: in all its forms an activity of the intellect, seeking Reality for its own purposes or those of humanity at large."[1] This may be often the case, but it is not inevitable that this should be so. There is, for example, no reason why the scientific and techno-logical skill of men should be abused and prostituted, except that men are self-centred. Miss Underhill says, "We are likely to fall victims to some kind of magic the moment the declaration 'I want to know' ousts the declaration 'I want to be' from the chief place in our consciousness."[2] Human nature being what it is, this is lamentably true. But there is no inherent reason why knowing and being should not be followed together—mind and heart be in unison, wisdom be conjoined to love.

It is commonly supposed that the only way of gaining knowledge and understanding of the world is through the exercise of mind in the fullness of its powers. That this is not the only way becomes clear from some of the mystical accounts which have been presented. There is much to show that the soul can, under certain circumstances, gather knowledge and wisdom, even though the mind is completely at rest. The mind is a very specialised instrument of knowledge and action—an indispensable instrument so far as the physical world is concerned. But there is a centre in the soul which can relate itself in mystical experience directly and immediately to that which lies behind appearance, thus intuiting this essence through and through. There were illustrations of this in Chapter 4. Jacob Boehme, the humble shoemaker, spoke for others than himself when he said, "The gate was opened to me, that in one quarter of an hour I saw and knew more than if I had been many years together at a university." The levels of Reality which we call Mind are by no means the *only* gateway to knowledge and understanding, but they are the only levels avail-

[1] *Mysticism*, p. 71 (Methuen & Co. Ltd., 1949 Ed.)   [2] *loc. cit.*, p. 151

able to most of us at the present time. Moreover, it is only by their use that we can express such knowledge in words or symbols for the benefit of others.

On the lower levels of Reality, saint and sage, mystic and occultist, can follow ways which are separate. There is a moral choice involved. A man may be a saint and have knowledge neither of the physical world in which he lives, nor of the powers of mind. Another man, a Hatha Yogi, may be able to walk over fires, swallow poisons with impunity, and levitate without difficulty, but he may possess no love for others and no saintliness of character. Happily, on higher levels of Reality, where mind as an instrument of knowledge is not essential, the two ways merge. Being and knowledge are linked together, and there is no way of understanding more except through being worthy to understand it. At this point the occultist has to come to terms with the mystic, and we can put into his mouth the words of Browning:[1]

> I too have sought to know as thou to love,
> Excluding Love as thou refused'st Knowledge,
> Are we not halves of one dissevered world,
> Whom this strange chance unites once more? Part! never;
> Till thou, the Lover, know, and I, the Knower,
> Love; until both are saved.

[1] *Paracelsus*

THE "UNCONSCIOUS" MIND

The root and origin of all the processes by which the life of men and
nature is determined is to be found in interior planes of being. Our minds,
while centred on our purely sensory experience are concerned only with
a region of outworkings, secondary processes and repercussions; the
originating causes are in an interior sphere. The visible is the derivative
and subordinate. Matter records and fixes but is powerless to create.

LAWRENCE HYDE

WE discussed in Chapter 4 the phenomena of one-ness and expansion,
and there expressed the view that these occur on various levels of
Reality. So much reference is made to the "unconscious" mind today
that it seems important to present our interpretation of it, especially
in relation to these various levels.

It is often supposed that the idea of an "unconscious" region of
the mind was wholly formulated by Freud, and developed later by
Jung and others. As early as 1887 F. W. H. Myers[1] was putting
forward the same conception. Myers wrote of "that supraliminal
current of consciousness which we habitually identify with ourselves",
and continued[2]

"I feel bound to speak of a subliminal or ultra-marginal consciousness
—a consciousness which we shall see, for instance, uttering or writing
sentences quite as complex and coherent as the supraliminal consciousness
could make them. Perceiving further that this conscious life beneath the
threshold or beyond the margin seems to be no discontinuous or inter-
mittent thing; that not only are these isolated subliminal processes comparable with isolated supraliminal processes (as when a problem is solved
by some unknown procedure in a dream), but that there is also a continuous
subliminal chain of memory (or more chains than one) involving just that
kind of individual and persistent revival of old impressions and response
to new ones, which we commonly call a self—I find it permissible and
convenient to speak of subliminal selves, or more briefly of a subliminal
self. I do not, indeed, by using this term assume that there are two
correlative and parallel selves existing always within each one of us.
Rather I mean by the subliminal self that part of the self which is

[1] Proceedings of the Society for Physical Research, Vol. IV, p. 256 (January
1887)
[2] Human Personality, Vol. I, pp. 14–15 (Longmans Green & Co. Ltd., 1903)

commonly subliminal; and I conceive that there may be—not only *co-operations* between these quasi-independent trains of thought—but also upheavals and alternations of personality of many kinds, so that what was once below the surface may for a time, or permanently, rise above it. And I conceive that no self of which we can here have cognisance is in reality more than a fragment of a larger self—revealed in a fashion at once shifting and limited, through an organism not so framed as to afford it full manifestation."

With reservations about the meaning of the last sentence, I think that C. G. Jung and most psychologists would agree with Myers—using the modern terminology of conscious and unconscious mind. I confess to a dislike of this terminology on the ground that it makes for ambiguity and confusion. Thus, Myers, in the passage quoted, wrote of "*conscious* life *beneath* the threshold" of consciousness. I quote now from Jung:

"Certain dreams, visions, and mystical experiences, however, suggest the existence of a consciousness in the unconscious. But if we assume a consciousness in the unconscious, we are at once faced with the difficulty that consciousness cannot exist unless there is a subject—an ego—to which mental contents are related. Consciousness needs a centre, an ego to whom something is conscious. We know of no other kind of consciousness, nor can we imagine a consciousness without an ego. Consciousness cannot exist when there is no one to say 'I am conscious'.

"I must admit that there are experiences that give plausibility to the hypothesis of an ego in the unconscious realm. Still, for the reasons already mentioned, I feel rather hesitant to adopt it, the more so as I should not know what or whom to call the ego of that consciousness." [1]

This passage illustrates how unsatisfactory a terminology it is which makes it necessary to speak of "a consciousness in the unconscious". My difficulty, however, is deeper than one of mere terminology. In the passage cited Jung has recognised the problem but not resolved it. Those of us who are prepared to recognise the existence of selves (both incarnate and discarnate) who can communicate telepathically with and through the subliminal mind of a subject, may claim that evidence of conscious intelligent purpose there is fully accounted for on *this* view. I believe a great many phenomena *are* accounted for in this way, and that these include works of an inspired character in poetry, art, music, etc., certain types of medium-istic trance, some dreams, and certain types of obsession and madness.

[1] *The Integration of the Personality*, p. 15 (Kegan Paul Trench, Trubner & Co. Ltd. 1940)

But I do not believe that all uprushes from the subliminal region which show evidence of purpose (such as an ego might account for), are to be explained in terms of the activity of external egos. A large proportion of a person's dreams, for example, is probably created within the psyche.

I believe it is possible to present a more satisfactory account of these regions of mind, and a more satisfactory terminology in which to describe the phenomena. As I have presented these views elsewhere,[1] the present account will be brief. The term "consciousness" suggests to many people a passive state—what William James called "inert diapheneity". We must remember, however, that it is more than this, for we can select what we choose to attend to. We replace it with *consciring* which is the *fundamental* activity of all sentients— from which all else derives. That which is conscired is called a *conscitum* (pl. *conscita*). The nature of consciring is closely akin to imagining. I do not refer to that feeble activity which gives rise to day-dreaming, but to the power which at its best is seen in the poet, musician and artist. Blake was constantly referring to this basic activity, as when he said "Nature is Imagination". Consciring and conscita, like imagining and the things imagined, are as inseparable as the two sides of a coin: one cannot exist without the other. Of course conscita of my consciring may themselves be sentients which conscire on their own account. Some primitive degree of consciring is considered to extend down the scale of being, even to electrons and protons. We distinguish between reflective and irreflective consciring. If an observing subject is aware not only of an object but of himself as aware of the object, this is reflective consciring. A dog may be aware of an object, but it is unlikely that it knows that it is aware of it. Its state is one of irreflective consciring. Human beings pass from reflective to irreflective consciring as they pass from the waking to the dreaming state. The permanent centre of consciring of human beings is to be identified with a centre in the soul, but there must be an outpost of this in the personality.

We have represented Reality (as in the diagram on p. 74) as existing on different levels. The region broadly labelled Mind is composed of many sub-levels or strata. In some of the higher of these, inspiration takes its source. Some of the lower levels are closely linked with physical organisms and endeavour to maintain them in a harmonious working condition. Very few of these processes can be reflectively conscired. (In popular language, we are not

[1] *Nurslings of Immortality*, p. 40 (Hodder & Stoughton Ltd., 1957)

"conscious" of them.) On some of these strata each individual mind must preserve its memory network. We know that a great part of our memories cannot be recalled at will. To account for the fact that some things are accessible to us at will, while others are not, we introduce the idea that there is a critical intensity threshold linked with each stratum. Conscita on this level can be reflectively conscired only if they are, or can be lifted in their intensity above this critical threshold value. Otherwise they are only irreflectively conscired. We assume that the intensity with which a particular conscitum can be conscired will be jointly a function of the centre of consciring and of the nature of the conscitum. In just such a way we may say that success in climbing a mountain is jointly a function of the strength and competence of the climber, and the height and other qualities of the mountain itself. It follows that contents of the psyche may be unavailable to reflective consciring for two different reasons. They may either exist on levels with a high critical threshold (on which the self, as it evolves, may sometime achieve reflective consciring), or, although on levels with a low threshold, the conscita may be intrinsically weak. (The so-called subliminal projection of which we hear today is an illustration of this.)

By the term "soul" we mean a permanently appropriated "body" or vehicle of the centre of consciring (which is itself Spirit). The soul de-limits and appropriates a specialised portion of the cosmic mind to be its own instrument. With the greater "amorphous" mind it retains, however, a relationship. The kind of relationship of which I think is that which a living cell retains with the tissue-fluids from which it is separated by a semi-permeable membrane. From the external "collective" mind there are energies and currents which are normally tolerable, continually diffusing inwards to the personal mind (and vice versa). Pursuing the analogy, it may be suggested that sometimes there is a temporary or permanent break in the boundary membrane which results in an invasion from the "collective" with which the personality cannot cope. Then there results one form of insanity.

Phenomena such as psychical epidemics, which hold a personality in their grip, represent such a breakdown, followed by mergence at some low personality level of the personal and the collective mind. We think of mob hysteria, of revivalistic meetings, of witchcraft trials, of dancing manias and the flagellation manias of the middle ages, of unsound investment booms, of fire-panics in theatres, and of occasional political stampedes. In all of these the personality is swept along by powerful emotional currents in the collective which he has allowed to invade himself. These things are called by Jung "perils of the soul". We should wish to substitute the term "personality" for "soul", for we do not hold that the soul is subject to these vicissitudes. The soul may, of course, fail to mature and gather wisdom; it may fail to achieve fully reflective consciring, for it depends largely on the successive personalities it creates to achieve this. But the possibility of failing in such a way is a different kind of peril.

We owe to Jung the concept of a collective "unconscious" in which is stored in archetypal forms the experience of the race. It is an important and valuable conception. The outlook which we present embodies this in a particular way. We believe that souls belong to groups which we have called Group-souls, and that the souls of any one group share a common or collective unconscious. This collective mind in its turn is de-limited from, but has relations with, a tribal or a racial collective, and so forth. Those who find similes helpful may picture a group of trees drawing their nourishment from an island in a lake. There are many islands, and all are linked with a greater whole which is the country to which the lake belongs.

Sometimes through dreams, visions, or motor automatisms, there is disclosed wisdom or insight or inspiration beyond that which the conscious self possesses. Where it appears to have come from within the psyche, we must recognise as possible sources (a) the intuitive wisdom which the soul has distilled from past lives and has made available to the personality and (b) the wisdom of other souls of the same group communicated through the collective mind which they share.

INADEQUACY OF PSYCHOLOGICAL POSTULATES

Broadly speaking, psychology claims that the psyche comprises a conscious part organised round an ego, and an unconscious part inaccessible to the ego. These, together with a collective unconscious, which is not personal, constitute the total reality within which all human experience is embraced and in terms of which it must be explained. The question with which we are particularly concerned is whether mystical experience can be accounted for satisfactorily within this scheme. (For the sake of making my position clear to the reader, I shall continue, with reluctance, to use the term "unconscious mind".)

Everything now hinges on what this term is understood to connote. If by it the psychologist understands the whole region of potential experience *of whatever kind* which happens to lie outside that boundary within which he can operate consciously—well and good. My objection in this case is to his presupposition that all which lies outside the conscious mind is necessarily of the nature of mind. I hold the view that there are certain higher levels of Reality which have characteristics so different from mind as we know it, that a new descriptive term is necessary. I call these levels collectively "Spirit". The difference is that which Plotinus recognised between the "sensible" and "intelligible" worlds.

If by the term "unconscious mind" the psychologist implies not only that the totality of experience can be accounted for in terms of "mind", but also that such mind is *itself* unconscious and is therefore more primitive or less evolved than conscious mind, I cannot see how all the data of experience can find an explanation. Such a view would allow an explanation of things like mass hysteria and psychical epidemics, but how would it account for the observation of Jung (which all workers in the field of psychical research would confirm)— "My psychological experience has shown time and again that certain contents issue from a psyche more complete than consciousness. They often contain a superior analysis or insight or knowledge which consciousness has not been able to produce" ? I state without hesitation that the data of mystical experience at their best are far beyond any possibility of explanation on such a hypothesis.

The confusion arising from the inadequacy of the concept of "unconscious mind" is clearly in evidence in the psychological commentary of C. G. Jung which is a preface to *The Tibetan Book of the Great Liberation*.[1]

Jung says, "Psychology holds that the mind cannot establish or assert anything beyond itself." If then a person makes a claim, based upon mystical experience, to have knowledge of certain metaphysical realities, psychology would have to say, "We cannot recognise the validity of your claim—but the fact that you make it at all interests us: there must be something in your unconscious mind to explain the fact that you do this." It is quite a gratuitous attitude to postulate that mind is all, and to say of man (as Jung does), "He has only to realise that he is shut up inside his mind and cannot step beyond it." Psychology has every right to say "We shall confine our study to mental function", but it must then honourably renounce

[1] W. Y. Evans-Wentz (O.U.P., 1954)

134

any claim to judge metaphysical truth. Unfortunately it does not do this. With its unsupported claim to be a *ne plus ultra* it proceeds to make judgments of metaphysical truth. "In the first place", says Jung, "the structure of the mind is responsible for anything we may assert about metaphysical matters." The reply to this is obviously that the mind may be responsible for the form of the assertion without being primarily responsible for the substance and fact of it. No one disputes the role of the mind in *communicating* experience, but in the light of our study of the data of mysticism, we shall repudiate any suggestion that the mind is its *fons et origo*. Every reader must form his own judgment on this issue. No one can *prove* that he is either right or wrong. But if sane and intelligent people are deluded in their unshakable conviction of the reality of the Truth, Goodness and Beauty which they have immediately and most convincingly experienced, or if such experience is to be attributed to the peculiarities of the unconscious, I can only say that we can count no expression of experience as a reliable pointer to truth, and we can trust no value-judgments. We may search in vain: all is vanity and vexation of spirit.

Such a hypothesis inevitably emasculates religion in that it recognises no God, no Reality to which man may aspire outside the great unconscious. It then becomes logical to say of faith that it "tries to retain a primitive mental condition on merely sentimental grounds. It is unwilling to give up the primitive child-like relationship to mind-created and hypostatized figures; it wants to go on enjoying the security and confidence of a world still presided over by powerful, responsible and kindly parents."[1] This may pass for faith with some people, but it is far from being an accurate or fair description of the healthy-minded and courageous attitude to life of a Schweitzer— which has achieved great things in the world.[2] However widespread may be the tendency to preserve mind-created and hypostatized figures, this tendency has no bearing on the existence of God or of any other High Beings.

The Eastern text on which Dr. Jung has written a psychological commentary is, as its name suggests, a mystical treatise dealing with Enlightenment or Illumination. A Western mystic, once he had familiarised himself with the unfamiliar Eastern terminology, would, I believe, understand it intuitively. The attempt of a psychologist to fit it into his conceptual scheme is most unconvincing. One of Jung's contentions, expressed as briefly as possible, is as follows:

---

[1] *loc. cit.*, p. xxxi   [2] St. Paul's assessment is found in Heb. xi

the conscious mental state is necessarily referred to an ego, since there cannot be awareness without someone who is aware. An egoless state means to Western thought an unconscious one. The East speaks of attaining high states such as Samadhi or Enlightenment in which the ego has gone or been dissolved. Therefore (says Jung) these states are equivalent to our collective unconscious. Such an astonishing conclusion might well have led the author to re-examine his premises; but no!—a little later in his commentary he says, "In the East there is the wisdom, peace, detachment, and inertia of a psyche that has returned to its dim origins . . ."[1] Again, he says, "The East cultivates the psychic aspect of primitivity,"[2] Dr. Jung is under a complete misapprehension in assuming that the alternative to ego-centricity is no ego. The observing centre of consciring is not lost: it is moved into union with the greater Spiritual Self in Enlightenment. The Western psychologist who has hypostatized mind can recognise no such Self, and for him all mystical experience must find its roots in the unconscious.

We have discussed in Chapter 4 the all-embracing sense of one-ness or unity which is very characteristic of mystical experience. What has Dr. Jung to say about this? "The extraordinary feeling of one-ness is a common experience in all forms of 'mysticism' and probably derives from the general contamination of contents which increases as consciousness dims . . . If we tried to conceive of a state in which nothing is distinct, we should certainly feel the whole as one."[3] Dr. Jung has claimed to be an empiricist and rather disowned the mantle of a philosopher. I find it difficult to understand, therefore, how he can put forward a hypothesis which so completely disregards a large amount of empirical data which points in the opposite direction. Let me remind the reader of statements which those who have had mystical experience have made.

"All at once, as it were, out of the intensity of the consciousness of individuality, the individuality itself seemed to dissolve and fade away into boundless being; and this is not a confused state, but the clearest of the clearest, the surest of the surest, the weirdest of the weirdest, utterly beyond word—where death was an almost laughable impossibility —the loss of personality (if so it were) seemed no extinction, but the only true life. I am ashamed of my feeble description." (Tennyson)

"I was seeing the significance of things . . . I had sensed great happiness, and a sureness of something that I felt was eternal life." (Case 5)

I invite the reader to look again through the mystical accounts of

[1] loc. cit., p. xlviii   [2] loc. cit., p. lv   [3] loc. cit., p. xlvi

Chapters 3 and 4. He will not find there a shred of support for Jung's suggestion that the mystic's "consciousness dims". On the contrary, he will find abundant evidence that the mystic's perception is enormously enhanced. He is infinitely more sensitive and aware than normally; *Light* and *Livingness* are frequently-used words. They speak, not of entering a foggy blurred state, but rather one of clarity and perfection. Without labouring the point further, it is obvious that Jung's suggestion that the sense of one-ness "derives from the general contamination of contents, which increases as consciousness dims" can only have a possible application to the one-ness which may occur on the lower levels of mind. This is the *participation mystique* referred to on p. 77, and this is not mysticism at all. Mystical experience lies quite outside any possibility of explanation in terms of modern psychology. In the words of Berdyaev,[1] "Mysticism belongs to the sphere of the spirit and not to that of the soul . . . it is, in a word, 'spiritual' rather than 'psychological'."

With a psychological approach to an essentially mystical document such as *The Tibetan Book of the Great Liberation* it is not surprising to find strange contradictions. I shall select only one example. We have been told that the unconscious is rich in content. "Whatever the structure of the unconscious may be, one thing is certain: it contains an indefinite number of motifs or patterns of an archaic character, in principle identical with the root ideas of mythology and similar thought-forms" (p. xlv). After assuring us that there can be no doubt about the identity of the term "One Mind" and the Unconscious, Jung paraphrases a passage thus, "The One Mind and the individual mind are equally void and vacuous." He comments, "Only the collective and the personal unconscious can be meant by this statement, for the conscious mind is in no circumstances 'vacuous'." (p. lxi)

Dr. Evans-Wentz, in his general introduction, makes it clear that by the One Mind is meant the "Universal All-Pervading Consciousness" which "alone is real". In other words it is synonymous with Absolute, or the Supreme Ground, or Godhead, from which all consciousness springs forth. If this is unconscious, as Dr. Jung[2] maintains, I conclude by saying, with regret, that words do not have the same meaning for us, and that between us there is a great gulf fixed.

---

[1] *Freedom and the Spirit*, p. 240 (Geoffrey Bles Ltd.: The Centenary Press, 1935)

[2] Dr. Jung's important little book *The Undiscovered Self* (1958) has just come to my attention. This represents a clarification of his position as it is at the present time, and I find myself substantially in agreement with it.

MADNESS

It is necessary to say something about the state of mind of those persons who are sometimes described as mad or psychotic. The necessity for doing so arises from the fact that the sense of expansion of mind—the experience of an all-embracing one-ness —is sometimes found in the schizophrenic and in the drug-taker as well as in the mystic, and this has led to some unwarrantable conclusions which I shall discuss later.

We are all being influenced, whether we like it or not, by the "collective unconscious". For example, archetypal figures occur in our dreams. Most of us are also influenced in some degree by currents of mass-emotion which play upon us from these levels. All this is, however, fairly continuous and within the norm. Outside the norm lie states of neurosis and psychosis. In general terms we may say that the neurotic person has to deal with factors which are repressed into the personal unconscious mind, and remains in a fairly normal relationship with his physical environment while doing so. The psychotic has to deal with serious and uncontrolled invasion from the collective unconscious, and does not remain in a normal relation with his environment which is interspersed with material from "within". Such a generalisation, while broadly true, should not be pressed too far. There are occasionally neurotic symptoms which seem to arise because of a resonant or reciprocal interaction between factors in the personal unconscious and the collective unconscious.[1]

It is not proposed to discuss psychosis in general, but to quote some of the views of John Custance who, in a very interesting book,[2] has described his own experiences over a period of twenty years as a manic-depressive. He passed through phases of elation which alternated with depression; normal phases separated these abnormal ones. He retained in memory vivid impressions of the latter. He writes:

"As the result of my experiences the whole universe has changed about me, and it will never be quite the same again.

"If I were asked to describe this change in the fewest possible words, I would say that the universe, the world of so-called material objects presented to my consciousness, came alive. At times in the depths of depression, it came alive with horrors as appalling as any visualised by medieval artists depicting Hell. If I stayed in bed, crumpled pillows,

[1] R. C. Connell and G. Cummins, *Healing the Mind* (Aquarian Press Ltd., 1957)
[2] *Adventure into the Unconscious* (Christopher Johnson Ltd., 1954)

folds of the bed-clothes, would take shapes suggesting unutterable evil; if I got up and went out, terrifying forms awaited me in every tree and bush. I could not walk through a wood, for example, without seeing, like Shakespeare's lunatic in *A Midsummer-Night's Dream*, 'more devils than great Hell can hold'. At other times, in periods of joyful excitement or elation, technically known as mania, the Kingdom of God seemed to come down to earth, bringing with it not only saints and angels, but the gods, goddesses and heroes of Olympus and Valhalla, of Carthage and Egypt and Babylon; there were elves and sprites in the trees and streams, fairies in the flowers; all things indeed were instinct with spiritual power and life. The kingdoms of the imagination had been opened to me; I had been in Hell and in Heaven; and the gates have never quite closed since . . .

"The world in which I found myself during those ecstatic moments, or rather periods—for the abnormal phases sometimes lasted for months—was, as I have just said, a world in which everything came alive. There was no such thing as an inanimate object, what the Jewish philosopher Martin Buber calls an 'it' as opposed to a 'thou'. Animate and inanimate seemed to merge one into the other; I could speak to all things, animal, vegetable and mineral, and all things could speak to me. Subsequently I have come to realise that this experience was almost precisely the same as that of the mystics; Plotinus put it in classic words: 'For everyone hath all things in himself, and again sees all things in another, so that all things are everywhere and all is all and each is all, the glory is infinite' . .

"Although I am far from being a saint it would be impossible for me to reject this other world as delusionary without at the same time writing off all mystical, or even all religious experience as nonsense."

In further description of the attractive phase of his experience, he says:

"In its favourable aspect it is a strange and lovely land beyond individuality and incidentally also beyond good and evil, since the opposites are reconciled and the peace that passes all understanding remains supreme. In it there is no death, no final separation, no fundamental or absolute division or distribution, no time, for all that ever was still is, now and for evermore."[1]

In trying to present the essence of wisdom which he distilled from his experience, Custance wrote:

"Am I only an individual? Or is my rather petty and irritating individuated personality merely one aspect of a vast unity transcending myself? That is, I think, how I would describe the basic conviction that I have retained from the strange experiences of so-called insanity. At the back of

[1] *loc. cit.*, pp. 2-4

my mind there is always the feeling that I am not only, not merely, John Custance, but, as it were, John Custance *plus* something else. And if I were pressed, as would only be reasonable, to say what this mysterious *plus* was, I would in the last resort define it as something that included everything that ever was or will be. It was Heraclitus who said that you could never come to the limits of the soul, for the soul had no limits. It is co-extensive with the universe itself."[1]

Let us examine his testimony carefully.

(1) He says, "the world of so-called material objects presented to my consciousness came alive." If the reader will refer to Chapter 4 he will find this livingness one of the most frequently reported features. Thus, in Case 19: "I instantaneously felt that every element of the landscape was alive, the light, air, ground and trees." Again, in Case 20: "Life, or spirit, call it what one would, was manifested variously in living things and in trees and air and stones." Case 22: "All became alive, the trees, the houses, the very stones became animated with life." Similar expressions are found in Cases 24, 25, 26, 27 and 29.

(2) Speaking of the ecstatic phase he said, "Animate and inanimate seemed to merge one into the other; I could speak to all things . . . and all things could speak to me." We find the same testimony in Chapter 4. The terms used there are "one-ness"; "everything seemed to be connected with everything else"; "the rocks, trees, etc. were I, I they—all brothers"; "identity with Nature wherein he functioned with and like Nature". All the cases given express this feature in their own way.

There can be no doubt that the pleasant aspect of Custance's experience tallies remarkably with that of the Nature mystics. In his further description of his state as "beyond individuality", and embodying the "peace which passes all understanding", without death, division or time, he is in harmony with the testimony of the mystics who are on the way to Illumination. His recognition of a place of reconciliation of the opposites differs in no important or significant feature from the experience of the mystics who realised a union of the self and the not-self.

What shall we say, however, of the depressive phase? It has no counterpart on the mystic way. It must not be confused with the "dark night of the soul" which is an experience of Western mystics who attempt to pass beyond the stage of Illumination. When Custance speaks of "horrors as appalling as any visualised by

[1] *loc. cit.*, pp. 5-6

medieval artists depicting Hell", and "shapes suggesting unutterable evil", Western man tends to shrug his shoulders and talk of a disordered mind, or of imagination running riot. This explains nothing. Is this world of evil and malevolent creatures wholly a subjective phantasmagoria, or has it objective reality on some level of which, fortunately, we have no conscious awareness as a rule? I think Jung would support the subjective view, for he characterised the schizophrenic as "a dreamer in a world awake". But even dreams, I would point out, do not all fall into one category: products of that creative and dramatising level of the mind which offers its fancies to another observing level. *Some* dream experiences can be best understood in terms of extra-sensory perception of the so-called etheric and astral levels of the world, to which must be attributed the same degree of objectivity as we ascribe to the physical world. We must be consistent in making a judgment on the issue. If the elated aspect of the experience of John Custance is, broadly speaking, awareness of the actual— having an objective existence apart from the individual observer— then we have no right to say arbitrarily that the depressive aspect is a mere subjective fiction. (I have used the qualifying phrase "broadly speaking" because the judgment of a finite observer may always be at fault, so that distortion or error may be superposed on data whether presented from within or without.) Some may suppose that when Custance speaks of perceiving "the gods, goddesses and heroes of Olympus and Valhalla, of Carthage and Egypt and Babylon" some errors of interpretation took place. It may be so, but for my own part, I think this approach is evasive. It leads one to ask what limits can be placed upon such supposed misinterpretation, and where we are to find criteria for truth?

I was interested to find in the unpublished account of a very intelligent man who passed through a psychotic experience a description which strongly suggested the character of higher "astral" levels. In this he says, "The upper air was peopled, though sparsely enough, both by the gods of classical antiquity and by the Christian angels."

My attitude to the problem raised is this. Wherever there has been a concentration of thought (strictly, *intense consciring*) by large numbers of people over considerable periods, there have been created permanent or semi-permanent structures or beings, which are perceptible to extra-sensory faculty. Gods and goddesses and mythical heroes, as well as less reputable beings, may indeed have an objective existence. Their status is not that of beings ensouled by a higher principle (i.e. possessing a centre of consciring), they are rather autonomous psychical systems although perhaps of considerable influence and permanence. Differentiation between such beings and so-called "real" ones is not necessarily easy for a sensitive as I have mentioned elsewhere in connection with the subject of apparitions.[1]

Let us return to the main question of the significance to be attached to Custance's experiences of the depressive phase. I do not think anyone questions the existence and prevalence of evil on our earth. Cruelty, greed, lust, anger and hatred are found everywhere in the affairs of men. Western man, who has given little thought to the matter, regards these things as undesirable "traits of character", or sins—and having thus labelled them, he is satisfied. If he has thought deeply about the psychical nature of the world he will be driven to recognise that these powerful evil energies of mind have objective existence on certain world-levels not far removed from the physical level. That they do not exist on higher levels of our world-structure is not the point; they are quite as actual as rocks and chairs and tables. In a living universe they find embodiment in forms, and they are to be reckoned with as such. Some of these forms are the so-called elementals, and where they embody evil they exist with lower types of discarnate human beings on the lowest "astral" levels (which constitute the "hell" of Christian orthodoxy). It is interesting to note that Custance himself, discussing both phases of his experience, makes the deliberate assumption that they are both actual. I agree with this assumption, and attempt to explain the two phases of his experience below.

The diagram on p. 74 may help us a little at this point. The experience of Custance has, of course, to do with the personality, not with the soul. Something akin to a breakdown of insulation of the personality from the collective mind takes place. The centre of consciring (or probably its representative in the personality) thus becomes aware of wide vistas on normally hidden levels of the world. The whole process of widened observation is complex, and I devote the next chapter to this subject. There must be many different modes of it, corresponding, perhaps, to the various levels at which breakdown may occur. When expanded awareness arises, what we experience does, I believe, depend on our moral and psychical development and our desires, latent or expressed. The evil in a man may draw him temporarily to lower levels, and the goodness may also draw him temporarily to higher levels. In the ordinary state of mind

[1] *The Imprisoned Splendour*, pp. 212-3 (Hodder & Stoughton Ltd., 1953)

this process is restricted and interpreted subjectively in terms of a mood. In the schizophrenic state of extended awareness, perceptions are clear and objectively interpreted. The door may be opened by various keys, but when this happens, the subject's experience will depend on what he is, on what he has the capacity to see, and on energies which may take control whether he likes them or not.

One recalls the observation which Dante once expressed so simply—that he felt he was rising into a higher circle because he saw the face of Beatrice becoming more beautiful.

THE ALL-IN-ONE EXPERIENCE

In discussing Nature-mysticism in Chapter 4 we observed that the sense of expansion into a wider field of awareness was found on different levels, ranging from the *participation mystique* of the lower ones to the union characteristic of mystical Illumination on the higher ones. The former expansion is commonplace in the primitive mind where it is used in all extra-sensory perception and in magical practices. When modern man contacts this level it is necessarily a submergence, and, for him, a regression. The depressive aspect of John Custance's experience was doubtless an involuntary contact with one aspect of this region. *If we wish to avoid confusion, it must be clearly recognised that the sense of one-ness occurs on different levels.* In general terms we shall affirm that there is nothing pathological about the experience of one-ness and expansion, for in a psychical universe we expect inter-penetration to exist. On the physical level it is least evident to us, but ascending through world-levels of increasing Reality it becomes a more marked feature. The mystic finds this as he climbs higher.

Professor R. C. Zaehner has written a scholarly book[1] in which he coins the term "pan-en-henic" for the experience of "all-in-one". Unfortunately he does not recognise that the pan-en-henic experience may be found on various levels. Regarding true mystical experience as necessarily theistic, *viz.* the Beatific Vision which leads ultimately to union with God, he has to find a place for Nature-mysticism. His way of doing so is one with which we are in complete disagreement. It is to disparage Nature-mysticism by associating it with lunacy and with mescalin-experience, and then put them all in the devil's basket. This theme echoes and re-echoes throughout his book. I shall quote a few examples out of many.

[1] *Mysticism, Sacred and Profane* (O.U.P.: The Clarendon Press, 1957)

Writing of Mr. John Custance he says:

"His case is interesting first because his experiences are so strikingly similar to those of Mr. Huxley when under the influence of mescalin, and to those of the Nature mystic who is sane, and secondly because there is no doubt that these experiences were solely due to his insanity. This establishes the awkward fact that, as Huxley clearly realised, there is a definite connection between Nature-mysticism and lunacy."[1]

He writes with approval of some of the early Muslim mystics who

"conceived mysticism like their Christian counterparts as an *askesis* leading to union with God in whose personal and unique existence they firmly believed; and they knew that this expansive experience which appeared to embrace all Nature, though not evil in itself, was a snare in their path: it was an 'insidious deception'. Christian mystics may well be referring to this experience when they speak of the Devil's ability to counterfeit mystical states."[2]

Again:

"In our study of Nature-mysticism we have been forced to the conclusion that this experience is, if not identical with the manic state in the manic-depressive psychosis, then at least is its second cousin."

It is curiously inconsistent to find Professor Zaehner, after such unflattering remarks about Nature-mysticism, writing:[3]

"When, however, these pan-en-henic experiences supervene spontaneously, there would seem to be no valid reason why they should not be accepted with gratitude. The experience is itself neither good nor evil . . ."

Professor Zaehner makes it quite clear that he regards the Nature-mystics (presumably when sane), as generally misled by their pan-en-henic experience into supposing that their experience is identical with that of the theistic mystics. Hence, he deduces, they must regard the terms "Nature" and "God" as interchangeable. I shall make one final quotation from his book:

"The confusion that is popularly made between Nature-mysticism and the mysticism of the Christian saints can only discredit the latter. By making the confusion one is forced into the position that God is simply another term for Nature; and it is an observable fact that in Nature there is neither normality nor charity nor even common decency."[4]

[1] *loc. cit.*, p. 51   [2] *loc. cit.*, p. 87
[3] *loc. cit.*, p. 104   [4] *loc. cit.*, p. 106

While I should be prepared to oppose anything discrediting the great mystical experiences of the saints, both Christian and non-Christian, I fear that Professor Zaehner has seen a "popular" confusion where none exists. Most of us are aware that there is an important distinction to be made between God manifested through Nature and immanent in Nature, and, on the other hand, the equation of God and Nature. There is a perfectly valid comparison possible between Nature-mysticism and theistic mysticism. In my judgment they are to be regarded as earlier and later stages of experience along the same road. They are related as are neighbouring foothills to the mountain peaks which they guard. Even better, we may suggest that they are related as communion with a poet through his works is related to communion with him face to face. Both are communion although there are far richer values in the latter than in the former. In his zeal to guard theistic mysticism Professor Zaehner has completely misinterpreted Nature-mysticism. He said,[1] "Communion with Nature is attainable without any effort, and without any moral perfection, without charity and even self-denial", but how can anyone know what the soul brings to this experience from its long past? This is an extraordinarily sweeping judgment. What a man says of communion with Nature depends on the man— Professor Zaehner or, let us say, Wordsworth. Francis Thompson spoke for almost all the poets when he said:

> One grass-blade in its veins
> Wisdom's whole flood contains.

But since, when Professor Zaehner looked he could see "neither morality, nor charity, nor even common decency", I shall select only Matthew Arnold to reply to him:

> One lesson, Nature, let me learn of thee,
> One lesson which in every wind is blown,
> One lesson of two duties kept at one
> Though the loud world proclaim their enmity
> Of toil unsevered from tranquillity,
> Of labour that in lasting fruit outgrows
> Far noisier schemes, accomplished in repose,
> Too great for haste, too high for rivalry.
> Yes, while on earth a thousand discords ring,
> Man's senseless uproar mingling with his toil,

[1] *loc. cit.*, p. 106

Still do thy quiet ministers move on,
Their glorious tasks in silence perfecting:
Still working, blaming still our vain turmoil,
Labourers that shall not fail when man is gone.

The first-hand accounts of Nature-mysticism which I have
presented in Chapter 4 may be left to speak for themselves. To me
they are the records of experience of men and women who have
stood on the foothills of spiritual Reality and breathed a clearer
air—above the mists of the valleys. They give us hints of great
snow-crowned peaks which have beckoned their spirits to adventure,
peaks with no discernible summits—inviolate in their mystery—
rising indefinitely into the blue.

Chapter

10

METHODS OF EXPANDING AWARENESS

Build thee more stately mansions, O my soul,
   As the swift seasons roll!
   Leave thy low-vaulted past!
Let each new temple, nobler than the last,
Shut thee from heaven with a dome more vast,
   Till thou at length art free,
Leaving thine outgrown shell by life's unresting sea.

O. W. HOLMES

IN this chapter I propose to write briefly of some of the methods used to liberate awareness from its normal limited field. In a few cases I shall illustrate what happens by first-hand accounts. I shall comment in particular on the drug-induced experiences which have created interest in recent years. The table below makes no claim to completeness. It attempts to classify into two groups some of the methods used, according as they are largely initiated on the physical level, or on the level of mind.

1. Hatha Yoga.	1. Mental Methods leading to forms of trance.	(a) Withdrawal. (b) Hypnosis. (c) Mantrams.
2. Exhaustion by Ascesis (fasting, vigils).		
3. Exhaustion by Dancing (Dervishes etc.).	2. Mind-and-Life Disciplines.	(a) Zen. (b) Raja Yoga. (c) The Mystic Way.
4. Insulation from Sensory Impressions.		
5. Anaesthetics.		
6. Drugs (Mescalin, LSD).		

It may be true that some methods predispose to expansion on low levels of mind, and that others favour higher experience of the mystical type. In evaluating the fruits of expanding awareness, we believe, however, that the method of inducing it is of small consequence compared with other factors such as the soul's inherent development and aspiration, and the motives and mood in which the adventure is undertaken. We know so little that it is probably unwise to make any generalisations.

The mystic way is a life-long discipline of thinking and being which one might suppose would constantly lead its devotees to higher levels. But there were numerous occasions when St. Teresa of Avila (and most of the other "classical" mystics) found themselves related to various mental levels where extra-sensory phenomena and levitations were in evidence. There were even times when she found herself in touch with lower astral levels, ascribing them, of course, in accordance with her own religious beliefs, to the devil. On the other hand, the taking of a drug or an anaesthetic may well appear to be a very prosaic stimulus, and yet it has sometimes led the person taking it to the levels of mystical experience.

PHYSICAL TECHNIQUES LEADING TO EXPANDED AWARENESS

I shall make only brief comment on the first four methods listed in the table. Hatha Yoga is an ancient Hindu system of disciplines which incorporates the practice of postures, a variety of breathing rhythms, and meditation. Its immediate aim is to bring under conscious control all physiological processes, so that the body as an instrument may function with maximum efficiency. Its ultimate aim is to arouse what is called "kundalini", a universal vital energy which is supposed to gain access to the body at the base of the spine. When aroused and controlled it is said to activate the psychic centres, and thus make available to the yogi paranormal faculty. It is claimed that if this energy can be directed to the head-centre (the thousand-petalled lotus), a blissful state is attained and the yogi becomes aware of "the great Consciousness that is God and which is in man". These practices are repeatedly claimed to be dangerous unless practised under the watchful eye of an expert. The serious student may consult Arthur Avalon's works on Tantric Yoga.

Ascetic practices have long been associated with religion in both East and West. Fasting, depriving the body of sleep, scourging the body, wearing hair-shirts, etc., have all had their devotees, and the ordinary person must often have wondered why. It seems probable that such ascetics frequently found compensations in experiences of a psychical nature, and (much more rarely), of a mystical nature. Others, on the other hand, deranged their nervous systems and became psychotic. In his book *Preface to Prayer* Gerald Heard has given a vivid picture of the Curé d'Ars whose ascetic practices over many years led to psychic phenomena—not the least interesting of which were the poltergeist effects. It is common knowledge today that those levels of ourselves which we distinguish as body and mind are so intimately related that to ill-treat the one is very likely to provoke unusual reactions in the other. One of the prisoners in a concentration camp in Hong Kong in the last war has left on record that in his extremely weak undernourished state he would sometimes rise from the sitting position and walk forward, only to discover, on looking back, that his body was still seated. The extreme weakness presumably facilitated involuntary astral projection. It is noteworthy that many of the records of spontaneous astral projection are associated with weakness of body due to illness or exhaustion, as well as to sudden shock.

The whirling Dervishes presumably pass into a state of mind which they do not find unpleasant, through the frenzy and physical exhaustion of the dance. The prevalence of the dance in tribal life among African peoples suggests that on many occasions it is used as a means of expanding consciousness through a primitive *participation mystique*.[1]

A very different kind of ill-treatment of the body-mind has been recently studied experimentally by Professor Donald Hebb[2] at McGill University. He tested human beings' ability to endure stimulus-starvation. The experimental subjects were placed in an air-conditioned chamber in silence, with opaque goggles over their eyes, and arm-restraints. Very few subjects could tolerate these conditions for more than twenty-four hours, and the limit was seventy-two hours. They produced emotional distress and hallucinations of seeing, hearing and touching. The visual hallucinations appear to have been elaborate changing geometrical patterns and fantastic moving imagery similar to that found through taking drugs such as mescalin or LSD. One man had a feeling of bi-location, presumably a limited form of astral projection. The account given does not describe expanded awareness so much as disorientated awareness, but these investigations are in their infancy. The sinister aspects lie in the discovery that after stimulus-starvation any information given to the mind is accepted uncritically. The subject has become highly suggestible and can be re-furnished with ideas, true or false. This so-called brain-washing can of course only affect the personality: the permanent self or soul is beyond any reach of man's villainy.

ANAESTHETICS

For a long time it has been known that under anaesthetics some people have had experiences of a mystical character. William James

[1] cf. Geoffrey Gorer, *Africa Dances* (Pelican Books Ltd.)
[2] *Discovery*, p. 93 (March 1957)

has recorded a number of these,[1] and referring to his own experiences he said:

"They all converge towards a kind of insight to which I cannot help ascribing some metaphysical significance. The keynote of it is invariably a reconciliation. It is as if the opposites of the world, whose contradictoriness and conflict make all our difficulties and troubles, were melted into a unity."

He quotes from B. P. Blood who wrote a pamphlet in 1874. "I know—as having known—the meaning of Existence: the sane centre of the universe—at once the wonder and assurance of the soul—for which the speech of reason has as yet no name but the Anaesthetic Revelation."

In his book *Diagnosis of Man*[2] Kenneth Walker quotes from an account of Sir Winston Churchill, who, in the spring of 1932, had an anaesthetic for a minor operation:

"The sanctum is occupied by alien powers. I see the absolute truth and explanation of things, but something is left out which upsets the whole, so by a large sweep of the mind I have to see a greater truth and a more complete explanation, which comprises the erring element. Nevertheless, there is still something left out. So we have to take a still wider sweep . . . The process continues inexorably. Depth beyond depth of unendurable truth opens."

The account which follows is an experience under light anaesthesia of a mother in childbirth:

"I was aware of being in another state of consciousness which was forced upon me by the pain and anaesthetised condition. The phrase 'ultimate reality' kept recurring, as if I was seeking the truth from the unknown. I gained the impression of an extraordinary plan (almost mathematical), down to the most minute detail. There was a sense as if truths were unfolding; my mind seemed as if it would float from truth to truth, or was opening up into new truths. It is difficult to find words to describe the experience. The plan I spoke of was incomprehensible, beyond the scope of our minds. My 'conscious' mind was restored on hearing the conversation of the operating staff. I heard Dr. R. say 'No good—nothing can be done about it.' This could easily have been interpreted as applying to the baby; yet I was not worried about it, as if part of me knew it was not about the baby. Finally Dr. R. gave the order to give me more anaesthetic . . . I was very relieved to see

[1] *Varieties of Religious Experience*, Lecture XVI (Longmans Green & Co. Ltd.)
[2] *Diagnosis of Man*, pp. 157-8 (Jonathan Cape Ltd., 1942)

the curtains on waking in my ward. The consciousness and recollection of being in another state were so strong that much convincing seemed necessary that I was back in a physical condition."

These two experiences indicate a contact with fairly high levels of mind. The case below appears to be one of astral projection.

"Many years ago while coming out of the ether after a serious operation I remember a nurse bending over me, asking my name, which had apparently not been recorded at the time of entry. Several times, in answer to her question, I replied, 'I haven't got a name'; at the same time, I myself—the real me—was quite detached from this scene, and I distinctly remember wondering in a tolerant amused kind of way, 'Who is this silly woman who says she hasn't a name?' Yet I knew simultaneously that this silly woman was myself, but I could not stop her speaking in this manner. The nurse finally gave up and went away."

The term "astral projection" covers obviously a variety of conditions[1] in which the centre of consciring divides its attention unequally between different levels of the self. The level which replied, "I haven't got a name" was clearly not much more than the near-physical levels of the body-mind complex (which conscires independently on its own account). A woman, B. E. B.[2] recognised this when she said:

"Under nitrous oxide gas for teeth, I am aware of nothing but the reluctance of bodily consciousness to be overcome. There is always a moment when an 'I' very distinct from the body gives the body orders to accept, and the body obeys. Dentists may say, 'You take gas well' but I am quite aware that this is because of the more seemly self taking charge of the bodily one."

The majority of persons who are given anaesthetics bring back no recollection of significant experiences, but there are some, as we have seen, who do bring back memories of expanded awareness. These memories range from what are little more than dreams to contacts with high levels of the Cosmic Mind where the sense of a great plan is dominant.

Through the kindness of the author I am permitted to reproduce here a remarkably full and valuable account of an experience under nitrous oxide.[3] The reader will notice a progressive awareness of

---

[1] *The Imprisoned Splendour*, pp. 220-9 (Hodder & Stoughton Ltd., 1953)

[2] Winslow Hall, M. D., *Recorded Illuminates*, pp. 80-1 (C. W. Daniel Co. Ltd., 1937)

[3] R. H. Ward, *A Drug-Taker's Notes*, pp. 26-31 (Victor Gollancz Ltd., 1957). This informative and interesting book deals chiefly with experience under LSD.

various levels of mind with a final emergence into the region of Imaginals accompanied by the Light which is characteristic of the union of soul and Spirit. It completes the first great stage of mystical experience: Illumination.

"On this occasion it seemed to me that I passed, after the first few inhalations of the gas, directly into a state of consciousness already far more complete than the fullest degree of ordinary waking consciousness, and that I then passed progressively upwards (for there was an actual sensation of upward movement) into finer and finer degrees of this heightened awareness. But although one must write of it in terms of time, time had no place in the experience. In one sense it lasted far longer than the short period between inhaling the gas and 'coming round', lasted indeed for an eternity, and in another sense it took no time at all. In terms of time, however, the first phase of the experience was comparatively brief (though perhaps it would be more exact to say that it was comparatively unimportant): a confusion of sensations in which, while I was already hardly aware of my body, I was still able to think in the ordinary way, and with some surprise that I was not being made unconscious by the gas I was inhaling, but very much the reverse. For already I knew, I understood, I actually was, far more than I normally knew, understood and was. I put it in this way because I had no impression of suddenly receiving new knowledge, understanding and being. Rather I felt that I was rediscovering these things, which had once been mine, but which I had lost many years before. While it was altogether strange, this new condition was also familiar; it was even in some sense my rightful condition. Meanwhile, what was becoming unreal, slow and clumsy was the ordinary world which I was leaving behind, but of whose shadowy existence I was still vaguely aware; indeed it presented itself to me as being like the receding shadow which fades across a landscape when the sun comes out.

"As for the emotional tone of this phase of the experience, I can only describe it as being compounded of wonder, joy and a wholly peaceful *inevitableness* for which there is no name. This sensation, which yet had nothing to do with my already anaesthetised senses, and to which our waking word-values do not belong, had an emotional depth which does not belong to waking sensation, so that it is all but indescribable. Meanwhile, the extraordinary feeling of *the rightness of things* increased, became more poignant, and was accompanied as it did so by a peculiar sensation of upward and bodiless flight. This sense of upward movement continued until it seemed to me that I was rapidly passing through what I afterwards told myself was a 'region of ideas'. The emphasis had shifted, that is to say, from the emotional to the intellectual.

"But it was only when I had 'come to' and was again subject to time as we know it that I felt that I had passed through this 'region of ideas' so rapidly that there had been no time to form concepts, to grasp anything of this region's content and store it for later reference, though in the midst of the experience itself there was all the time in eternity; and, besides, concepts were quite unnecessary in that part of consciousness, since one could manage perfectly well without them: this was a condition of complete and spontaneous lucidity, where there was not the slightest need to 'think'. One simply knew; and one knew not one thing here and another thing there, and all of them things quite unknown to ordinary consciousness; one knew everything there was to know. Thus one knew also that everything was one thing, that *real knowledge* was simultaneous knowledge of the universe and all it contains, oneself included. It was perfectly true, what one had read in the books; in reality (as opposed to the comparative unreality in which we live) the All is the One . . .

"In the 'region of ideas' everything lived and moved; everything 'breathed', but breathed with that 'one breath' which is the universal inspiration and expiration expressed in the cardinal opposites of day and night, male and female, summer and winter. Indeed the wonderful and awe-inspiring livingness of everything seemed to be part of the interrelatedness of everything; within the one thing which the entire universe was, the multitudinous aspects of it enjoyed a living relationship both to one another and to the totality, and this in an extraordinary complexity which at the same time was an extraordinary simplicity. According to our ordinary way of understanding we are used to relating to one another only things between which a relationship is sensually perceptible or logically calculable. Here relationships were of a different kind altogether. Things were related to one another which to ordinary thinking would have no connexion whatever, and related to one another in ways which we cannot normally conceive. Things which we should call far apart, whether in space or time or by their nature, here inter-penetrated; things which we should call wholly different from one another became one another . . .

"One knew and understood this different world as a spectator of it, recognising it as the object of one's apprehension, but at the same time knew and understood that it existed within oneself; thus one was at once the least significant atom in the universal whole and that universal whole . . . Meanwhile, the 'bodiless upward flight' continued. The 'region of ideas' gave place to another of which I can only say that in it everything came to rest in a perfection of light. Here, while all was certainly living, all was unchanging. Here *at the heart of the sun* stillness had its being . . . And the light in which one found oneself and which one called 'the sun', was of an utterly indescribable purity and lucency. It was as if the gathering momentum of the 'flight' of the unconscious dental patient into consciousness, which had become faster and faster through the 'region of ideas', had now reduced those multitudinous ideas by an incalculable

153

series of combinations and cancellings to this final and perfect unity. In the 'region of ideas' one had understood that this must be so. Now it was so . . .

"Thereafter the upward flight became a downward flight; whereas one had risen into the pure light of the sun, now one fell again towards the shadows of earth. I was once more aware of being in the 'region of ideas', and this time, as consciousness diminished towards the consciousness of everyday life . . . the 'region of ideas' took form; on its nether fringes the symbols we need in the waking state if we are to comprehend 'intuition' were supplied. In a flash, as it seemed to me, *I saw the meaning*; the meaning, that is, of the universe, of life on earth, and of man. As the darkness of what we flatter ourselves is consciousness closed in upon me, and even as I began dimly to be aware that I was 'coming to', the sum of things appeared before my inward eyes as a *living geometrical figure*, an infinitely complicated and infinitely simple arrangement of continually moving, continually changing golden lines on a background of darkness. (Geometry, it has often been recorded, is a common form for such visions to take.) These golden lines were all that was left of the pure lucency of the 'region of light', yet, mere shadows of that original glory, they still conveyed something of its perfection. This living geometrical figure seemed to be telling me that *everything is in order*, that everything works according to an ineluctable pattern, and that, since all things are under the sun's almighty eye, nothing need ever be wholly meaningless, even on earth, where we live so far from the central and perfect unity. Provided that we bear the pattern's existence in mind, even pain (of which my body was already beginning to be aware) can have meaning; so can death; so can the worst that we may have to endure; while the possibility of discerning this meaning is itself the meaning of divine mercy.

"By now I was sufficiently aware in the ordinary sense to feel myself as something separate from this geometrical design which was a representation of the sum of things. I was once more able to think normally, to say to myself as the golden lines faded, 'So that's what it all means', and even as I said it to forget what it all means; I had 'regained consciousness' and with it an aching jaw and a vague impression of the dentist impatiently telling me to pull myself together. Yet a dim and apparently nonsensical echo of 'what it all means' did remain in my head. 'What it all means', I was urgently telling myself in the attempt to frustrate the swamping forgetfulness, is 'Within and within and within and . . .' repeated like a recurring decimal."

This anaesthetic experience took the participant through to the high level of Illumination, and the brilliant descriptive writing of Mr. Ward has given us one of the most valuable accounts I have read.

PSYCHEDELIC DRUGS: MESCALIN, LSD ETC.

For a long time men have known of the existence of drugs which will produce profound changes in thought and feeling without involving loss of touch with the physical world (as in anaesthetics). Some are dangerous and habit-forming; others, such as mescalin, lysergic acid diethylamide and others, are non-addictive, and, taken in a proper dose, harmless. Their physiological effects are small, but they have remarkable effects on the mind, and the term "psychedelic" or "mind-manifesting" has been suggested as an appropriate one by Dr. Humphry Osmond. These drugs are of considerable interest to psychiatrists because they mimic temporarily some of the features of schizophrenia, and the term psychotomimetics has been used to describe them. Dr. Osmond's term is preferable because the experiences under the drug, and the implications of these, are far wider than those implied in a "mimicry of psychosis". They reach out into psychology, sociology, philosophy, psychical research, art and mysticism. We shall only here concern ourselves with the changes in perception and the opening of a door to exploration of higher levels of the world.

When 400 milligrammes of mescalin or 0·1 milligrammes of LSD are taken orally, symptoms of disturbed perception usually begin within half an hour to an hour. They rise to a crescendo and substantially subside in about eight hours. I shall briefly refer to experiences of a few who have taken these drugs, pointing out that not every taker would experience all of these, nor would he necessarily experience the same things on different occasions. Many factors appear to influence a particular group of experiences under the drug's influence: the quality of mind and character, the dominant interests, the willingness to "let go", the mood in which the experiment is entered upon etc.[1]

Ordinary objects become strangely significant and meaningful. "In the many thousand stitches of a well-worn carpet, I saw the footprints of mankind plodding wearily down the ages. Barbed wire on a fence outside was sharp and bitter, a crown of thorns, man's eternal cruelty to man." A sparrow, a faded carnation, any small thing might lead to profound absorption and seem worth a lifetime's study.

Sense perception grew in vividness, in intensity and sharpness,

[1] Humphry Osmond, *On Being Mad* (Saskatchewan Psychiatric Services Journal, July 1952)

but also became "infinitely more fluid and changeable". Perspectives would change, faces would alter grotesquely, and both the sinister and the beautiful would appear and disappear. A hand would seem "shrunken and claw-like", a recording machine would start to glow until the heat became overwhelming.

With the eyes closed brilliant visions would be seen. "Showers of jewels flashed across this inner vision, great landscapes of colour spread out before me, and almost any thought would be accompanied by a vision which was often supernally beautiful." Language was wholly inadequate to describe these "enchanting mindscapes".

The quality of the surroundings could, however, never be relied upon, for walls might tremble menacingly, "a twisted string might suddenly become a snake, and if I became panicky, would writhe towards me". A slight difference of opinion between two persons present resulted in "the room which had been brilliantly lighted becoming dark, the colours losing some of their vitality, and I felt her criticism of him as a bitter taste, an acrid smell, an ill-localised pain". One might summarise these effects as ever-changing qualities of feeling and perception, intermingled with hallucinations and delusions.

In an account of his own mescalin experience Christopher Mayhew[1] also described changed perspectives and fascinating colour phenomena, but he was particularly impressed by two phenomena linked with time. The first of these was that events which happened during the afternoons were experienced, not in the normal time-sequence, but haphazardly. Sometimes the *same* events were experienced with an equal degree of reality more than once. It was as though the events of the afternoon co-existed, but that under the influence of the drug he did not move steadily through them in one direction, but capriciously among them. The second odd experience was that on several occasions he lost awareness of his immediate surroundings for periods which could only have been seconds, but which to him seemed vast tracts of time of the order of years. These were, moreover, blissful excursions. In recollection, the afternoon seemed best described as "countless years of complete bliss interrupted by short spells in the drawing room".

In the first LSD experiments described in his book, Mr. R. H. Ward also reported the apparently strange behaviour of time. On one occasion he observed his hand growing steadily smaller, and he describes the terror which seized him as he endeavoured (success-

[1] *The Observer* (Sunday, October 28th, 1956)

fully) to arrest and reverse the process. An even more startling experience was when he looked at his face in the mirror and observed it simultaneously grow younger into a child's face and older into that of an old man. Of the two simultaneous changing appearances he says that "these movements in opposite directions were really one movement in a direction unknown to us". Perhaps it was into the same unknown direction that Mayhew slipped for years of bliss. I do not think anyone would venture, in our present state of ignorance, to offer any explanation of these strange relationships between the human mind and time. Ward's six experiments were varied in their atmosphere, and his commentary is of great interest and value. He closed the series because they were becoming repetitive in detail, and he felt they had taught him, for the time being, all that he desired to know of his own inward state.

In contrast with the above accounts there is given below the experience of a University professor which reaches the mystical level. Professor H. attached some importance to previous discussions in a seminar which led him to say,

"I had been induced to look at the evidence for the existence of certain psychic phenomena, and found it much better than I imagined. I had never experienced anything in the religious area that amounted to more than an aesthetic appreciation of nature, but intellectually I had been quite impressed with the uniformity of reports of mystical experience . . .

"By way of more immediate preparation, I had taken the 30/70 carbon dioxide/oxygen mixture several times. In doing this I had discovered the necessity of completely abandoning oneself to the experience. Any desire to 'run things' or any fearful reservations resulted in mild physiological effects without significance. The last time, however, I attempted to convince myself that whatever happened in the experiment, even including death, was all right. I tried to embrace the experience, whatever it was to be. This time I seemed to see a bright white light at the end of a long tunnel, and had an intense feeling that it would be wonderful if I could only reach it. I couldn't get to it before the effects of the gas wore off, but I felt very excited and exhilarated. This effect lasted to some extent for a day or two. I had the feeling that the light represented something very important and that I must reach it. (This of course was a feeling only—my rational mind was telling me this was just an interesting vision with no significance.)

"I took the material (100 microgrammes) at 7.20 p.m. There was practically no reaction for about half an hour; then I began to notice minor effects. Things appeared to be a little out of proportion—my hands, for instance, appeared unduly large.

"Everything seemed inordinately funny, and I had periods of hilarious laughter. I was a little bothered by not having control of the situation—I didn't feel my hands or my tongue would respond properly. I laughed on and off until about 8.45 p.m. and remarked, 'I hope I don't spend the whole evening laughing.'

"I felt tingly all over by this time, and also felt a little conspicuous as the centre of attention of eight other persons. I went into the bathroom and was captivated by my image in the mirror, which was quite radiant. Everything in the room looked a little more vivid and different somehow, but not enough so to really keep my attention.

"I sat down again and M. suggested that I listen to the music and try to let go and just drift off with it. I agreed to try this, with remarkable results. I saw a rapid succession of beautifully coloured images—fantastically beautiful and brilliant. Some looked like jewels, others were gorgeous sprays of vivid colour, still others were in the form of geometrical designs. This exciting panorama fascinated me for quite a while, and it was 9.30 p.m. when I reported back to the group. I told M. I had been waiting for him to do something, and now realised I must do it myself.

"One of the persons in the group asked if it would bother me if she smoked. I replied that I would rather she didn't. I said I didn't know why—it was just a feeling. 'Everything important is feelings,' I added as an afterthought. It seemed a very meaningful remark, and shortly afterwards I broke into uncontrollable mixed laughing and sobbing. I hid my face with a handkerchief so the group couldn't watch. 'I'm not sad, really I'm not,' I told them, 'I'm just getting out feelings I haven't been able to all my life. Don't pity me.' The sobbing changed back to laughter again. 'It's so funny. I feel as though all these feelings had been bottled up inside, and someone just took the stopper out.' Someone asked how I felt about the group watching me, and I realised it was no longer important—I didn't care if they watched me cry. 'I don't give a damn about you,' I replied. Someone asked about my being concerned about the opinions of others, and I answered that was in the past—it was cleared up now.

"It was now about 9.45 p.m. and I had become conscious that R. was in an attitude of silent prayer. But very strangely, I was aware that I could somehow sense her presence even when I was looking in a different direction or had my eyes closed. I felt drawn away by her, with a force that seemed almost material. Someone asked another question but I declined to answer. 'I want to do R.'s experiment: now quiet!'

"The remaining portion of the experience is extremely difficult to describe. I found that 'I' was completely detached from my body and free to wander at will. 'I' was floating in faintly blue and vast space, congruent with ordinary three-dimensional space, and yet somehow off in another dimension.

"Furthermore I was not alone. R. (who was now in a state of deep prayer) was there with me. I sensed her presence as a darkness in the blue space and as a force. In addition there was a third presence which I could neither see nor feel, but knew was there. I knew this third presence was God. (Up to this time I had used the word God in conversation very little, and always felt a little uncomfortable with it. I looked upon God as a hypothetical construct more than something one could directly experience. Thus I was quite surprised to find myself recognising this unfelt and unseen presence.) I could feel the force of R. leading me on, insisting that I go on.

"From time to time I reported back to the group briefly. 'There is no doubt of mental telepathy. I can read R.'s mind. I know just what she is thinking. This is fantastic. R., God and I have a dance going on up here. She doesn't approve, but I'm going to tell you about it. I'd like to tell you what is going on and bring the rest of you into this, but R. says there is more to be done first.' (11 p.m.) . . .

"At this time I was hovering about ten feet above my body and could 'see' perfectly clearly the group sitting around below, engaged in their silly pursuits. 'It's important that you know this is really going on. I am in closer touch with R. than if we were sitting here talking with one another.' I was attempting to convince the group of what I still have a deep conviction is so, that this experience was no illusion or hallucination (like the earlier coloured visions) but was perfectly real. This account is being written several months after the experience, and a considerable amount of reality-testing has gone on; yet the conviction persists that this experience and that which follows were not illusion . . .

"It was by now about midnight. I was more conscious than ever that R. was urging me on to see more. She was pushing me upward, upward. I thought I could also feel faintly a force from the rest of the group, but I wasn't sure. Then I was caught in the updraught of a powerful force and went soaring up toward a light that had appeared. I knew it was the same light that I had seen in the distance with the gas. But this time I made it! I could feel the outstretched arms of R. buoying me upward from below, and then the pull from above lifted me beyond what she could reach, and I was alone, utterly alone, completely detached from all I had ever considered 'real', and in the presence of the reality behind the 'real'. I was supported and enveloped by a pinkish cloud of light, and I knew this is the source of all love and beauty and goodness. I was filled with boundless, indescribable joy; enraptured with beauty, electrified with the currents of love pouring through me.

"I had no desire ever to leave this state of envelopment in the warm love of God. How long I remained there I had no idea: time has no meaning there. From being present with others when they experienced the same thing I realise it was probably a matter of no more than a few seconds by our time scale.

"Shortly after this I announced to the group that I thought the effects

159

of the material were wearing off, that it was all over. I recognise now that
there was much more which could have been done in extending my
awareness of the nature of reality, had someone in the group been experienced enough to act as director. It was as though I found myself in a
strange new land, and was too bewildered to go exploring without a guide.
It was safer to remain in the railway station and wait for the return train,
even though I knew from looking at the limited view through the window
that exploration would be fascinating and instructive.

"I reported to the group that what I had learned I would not have
learned without R.'s prayerful assistance—that, without this, the evening
would have been wasted. 'R. was teaching me to pray all evening' seemed
to sum up the experience. (12.45 a.m.)

"Looking back at this experience after several months, and having in
the meantime observed a number of LSD sessions with other subjects,
I find that the conviction of the reality of this other world and of a God
that can be contacted is a growing rather than a diminishing conviction.
. . . I have been privileged to experience briefly and incompletely an
aspect of the deeper reality. Like a traveller who has spent but an hour
in a strange land, I could describe very little of it. Yet I know, absolutely
and finally, that reality exists behind the material universe we perceive
with our senses; that man potentially has the power to perceive this
reality; that in this reality is a Source of love and goodness which man
potentially is able to contact and draw from; and that the extent to which
a person realises this potentiality is the most important fact about his
life."

In response to enquiry of Professor H. as to whether R. had any
corresponding perception on her part, I was informed that she was
a person who had developed the ability to cross without aid those
thresholds which LSD helps others to cross: that "she had proceeded
part way through the levels of prayer as described by the great
masters such as Poulain". "In her description," says Professor H.,
"she spoke of being 'out there', and suddenly, I was 'out there' with
her. This was a direct simultaneous perception of both of us, as
though one mind were infused with the other. I have experienced
this same thing with another individual under LSD, on another
occasion. It is a non-verbal but very positive form of communication
which depends on no verbal cues or other sensory perception as
nearly as we can tell. I feel quite certain it could take place between
persons in different rooms, for instance."

Commenting on this very interesting and informative account,
I draw the reader's attention to the sequence of experiences which
disclose the levels of mind affected. Observe, first, the disturbance of

normal sense-perception, then vivid hallucinations of the visual-colour type, then great emotional release—a therapeutic phase; out-of-the-body experience followed, with a vivid sense of mind-to-mind communication, and, finally, a passage "upwards" to a level of "the reality behind the 'real'". Description of the highest phase is similar to that of mystics drawing near to Illumination. The sense of 'I' remained so that the journey was not completed, but in essential points the account can rank with several of those in Chapter 3. The summing-up of Professor H. is impressive testimony to the value of the psychedelic drugs if carefully and wisely used.

IMPORTANCE OF THE PSYCHEDELIC DRUGS

(1) These drugs are of interest to the psychiatrist, and some research is taking place at present in this field.[1] They can be used to produce what is called a "model psychosis"—for a limited time—so that the condition can be studied. It is quite a possibility that a form of chemo-therapy may emerge from this work. There are close chemical affinities between mescalin and adrenalin (a naturally occurring body substance), and research is proceeding into the possibility that certain derivatives of adrenalin may be a cause of schizophrenia.

(2) The drugs offer to psychiatrists and skilled workers in the field of mental disorder the possibility of first-hand experience of the mental states in which psychotics are imprisoned.

(3) Since under certain conditions there is evidence of emotional release and also of the development of insight into mental conflict and stress, these drugs may have a useful place in certain types of psycho-therapy.

(4) The drugs may prove a useful means of undertaking experimental psychical research. Professor H. was convinced of his mental rapport with R. in the experience described. Others have reported similar experience under the drug's influence. Dr. Osmond has written to me:

"I think we *may* now have agents which, if properly and carefully used, will enable those who are not normally either psychic or sensitives to have similar experience to them. We have naturally got to make very careful enquiries to learn how to develop suitable methods. It is not just a matter of taking LSD or mescalin. One has to learn *how* to do it, just as one learns how to use any other instrument—for they are highly specialised

---

[1] e.g. Humphry Osmond, *A Review of the Clinical Effects of Psychotomimetic Agents* (Annals of the New York Academy of Sciences, Vol. 66, p. 418, 1956/7

instruments for changing the manner in which the brain works. Astronomy is not just a matter of having a telescope. When used properly LSD 25 appears to allow communication of a complex non-verbal sort to occur, and also allows one to contact what seem to be much higher levels of personality. If we can substantiate this it means that we shall not have to rely on rarely occurring mediums and sensitives. My impression is that one of the greatest troubles is that only very rarely is the medium's mind-brain apparatus at all suitable for carrying the highly complex ideas which could come down from higher levels. Consequently the ideas are more or less distorted and diluted—rather like a radio receiver which was taking in a symphony concert but was insensitive to about half the sounds. Clearly, if we can teach scientists to be sensitives we shall get on much more quickly."

(5) Experience under the psychedelics may have an important contribution to make to Art. One of the characteristics of the good artist is his ability to observe more carefully and deeply than the ordinary person, and to feel as a consequence more significantly. There is almost unanimous testimony from those who have taken these drugs that commonplace things acquired enormously enhanced significance, and that magnificent displays of force and colour were perceived. Dr. Ian Stevenson says, "The intensity of the colours and the fascination with colours and shapes which many subjects experience, leave an unforgettable residue of appreciation for the beautiful.[1] Dr. Osmond writes "Most subjects find the experience valuable, some find it frightening, many say that it is uniquely lovely . . . Our subjects include many who have drunk deep of life, authors, artists, a junior cabinet minister, scientists, a hero, philosophers, business men. For myself, these experiences have been the most strange, most awesome, and among the most beautiful things in a varied and fortunate life. They are not escapes from, but enlargings, burgeonings of reality."[2]

Most of the accounts of drug-induced experience refer to the visual imagery, but if the artist were one whose medium of expression was music or poetry it is possible that he might find inspiration in audible form. It is clear from several accounts that the higher levels of mind possess a comprehensive faculty of apprehension: it is only on the lower levels that this is broken down into sensory channels.

(6) The psychedelic drugs should hold much of interest for other groups of students, among which would be philosophers of both

---

[1] Journal of Nervous and Mental Disease, Vol. 125, p. 439 (1957)
[2] loc. cit.

idealist and realist views. Our principal concern, however, is their significance for the religious aspirant. It has been suggested by Aldous Huxley,[1] Osmond, Slotkin,[2] and others, that the drugs may have value in building-up empathy in a group-fellowship, thus bringing into existence a vital communion on levels of thinking and feeling. This is something which religious groups hope to achieve by their ritual, but seldom do in any marked degree. We are told that American Indians who use peyotl do in fact achieve this.

The aspect of greatest interest for us is how far a person desiring mystical experience may find help on his spiritual journey through using these drugs in a wisely directed manner. Such a possibility has seemed shocking to some people, as though it were an attempt to find a spiritual short-cut, or obtain something for nothing. It has been suggested that if it were possible it would "make nonsense of all contemplative religion". This, expressed briefly, is Professor Zaehner's position. It is natural that, with this pre-judgment, he should seek to establish that drug-induced experience is necessarily something different from that of the theistic mystics. In his book *A Drug-Taker's Notes*, Mr. R. H. Ward compares his experiences under LSD with those of a friend A, who had a mystical experience of a deeply-moving character. The difference between his own experiences and A's experience was, in his view, "highly important". He considered that something was missing from the drug-experiences which could only be called "the knowledge and love of God". No one would wish to dispute Mr. Ward's judgment of his own experience, but it is another matter to endorse his generalisation about *all* drug-experiences on the one hand, and natural mystical experience on the other, that "in spite of their similarities, the two kinds of experience cannot ultimately be compared"—that God is absent from the one type and present in the other. In the light of experience such as that of Professor H. this is not true. Moreover, Mr. Ward's anaesthetic experience was of the genuinely mystical type, and so are others which are on record.[3] If one may say so without irreverence, is God partial to anaesthetics rather than drugs —to chemicals absorbed into the respiratory tract rather than those taken into the alimentary tract?

Why should it be thought any more unfitting that true mystical experience might follow the taking of a drug, than if a man took an

[1] *The Doors of Perception* (Chatto & Windus Ltd., 1954)
[2] Transactions of the American Philosophical Society, Vol. 42, Pt. 4 (1952)
[3] William James, *The Varieties of Religious Experience*, Lect. XVI

anaesthetic and mystical experience followed it, or than if he did nothing which might be regarded as causal and yet mystical experience was granted? Mystical experience is no commonplace or frequently occurring thing, drugs or no drugs, and the soul that enjoys it is properly assumed to be worthy of it. There are no short-cuts to mystical experience, and it is difficult to understand how the possibility of mystical experience under drugs could ever have been deprecated as "making nonsense of all contemplative religion", except on the naïve assumption that taking the drug might be the sole, or chief, causal factor of mystical experience. What the drug does is to liberate, in varying degrees, the attention of the observing centre "from its biological focus to an extraliminal one".

With Dr. Osmond's permission I quote some views which he has expressed to me in personal letters.

"My guess is that there is no essential difference between the mescalin experience (and that of similar substances), and the mystical experience. They are part of a continuum. The absence of spontaneity in the experience has less to do with its value than whether the mind is open or closed, whether the soul is ready or not. Other important factors are capacity (and wish) to verbalise the experience, and a social setting in which it is accepted and acceptable. Very few people do not find the experience hugely significant, although some don't like it. They are frightened either by themselves and their own subconscious, or by an unexpected aspect of other people's experience . . . Some go right out to the One, the ineffable and unspeakable."[1]

"My present feeling is that there are a great variety of LSD and mescalin experiences depending on the personality of the taker, his experience of the new medium, and deeper factors which we don't understand yet. We should be wary of dogmatising. All the LSD does is in some way to put the brain partly out of action so that one can be in two places at the same time. What we need now are technical methods of focussing this marvellous display of mind, so that we can increase our understanding. As I see it there are two unopposed ways of advancing. For the saints there is direct communion. For the rest of us who are not yet ready, there is an expansion of mind, leading (one hopes) to what will be an evolutionary jump in which much of our symbolic communication (very clumsy) will be replaced by direct mind-mind communication. With this must go an expansion of Love and Tolerance—since, if we don't do this, it looks as though we will either go out with the bang of the fission bomb or the whimper of radiation sickness."

[1] A friend who is a mystic writes, "The mystic responds to deepening degrees of awareness by giving himself to what he becomes aware of. We have to jump, not only look on, before the Hand-from-Above lifts us up."

"It seems most necessary to differentiate clearly between the technical procedures . . . and the spiritual enlargement then available, to those who wish for such enlargement. It is the absurd muddling of these very different matters which plagues us at the moment. The well-fed modern white, kept aseptic by constant medical care, is extremely unlikely to develop transcendental experience of any sort by modern prayer techniques unless he is very anxious or pre-schizophrenic. Starved, exhausted, deprived of sleep, entombed, he may. But his very high vitamin and protein diet makes it hard for him. Some few unusual people are much more susceptible—but socio-culturally and dietetically we are heavily insulated against it. It is doubtful whether starvation is a suitable technique —most of us get too anxious that way. We are a food-conscious culture. Owing to our excellent diet we would have to do far more starving than our ancestors . . . LSD is an instrument: well-used it enlarges experience . . . It stops the explorer of the self and the soul using up all his energy to explore, and so valuing this stage almost as highly as the experience itself . . . It may make it possible for many of our best and most alert minds to have glimpses of the Unknown and so make us aware of its overwhelming importance."

MENTAL TECHNIQUES LEADING TO EXPANDED AWARENESS

In a frequently quoted passage William James expressed his conviction that "our normal waking consciousness . . . is but one special type of consciousness, whilst all about it, parted from it by the filmiest of screens, there lie potential forms of consciousness entirely different." We should express the same conviction in different terms: given the necessary stimulus we can transfer reflective consciring from the usual level to others on which we normally conscire irreflectively.

Normal perception is perception on one particular level of the world. In psychometry or object-reading the mind becomes aware of another level of the world possessing a different quality. A piece of stone is no longer just a definite object occupying a certain space: it is rather a field of qualities extended in space and time, and linked with every mind-body which has been in a significant relationship with it. Whenever the mind is withdrawn from its close but limiting association with the organs of sense, an expansion of awareness called extra-sensory perception becomes possible. (With Bergson, we regard the brain as an organ of limitation from a sensory viewpoint, and essentially designed for the facilitation of action.) There are various modes and degrees of withdrawal from the normal waking state, and we know very little about them. There is substantial evidence of an "astral" body or vehicle in which the mind functions when withdrawn partially or completely from the physical body, and I incline to regard what we call extra-sensory perception as an imperfect form of what we should describe as normal sensory perception if we functioned in an astral body. The reader will recall that there was evidence that mystical experience was sometimes preceded by astral projection.[1]

Of hypnosis I shall say very little. I do not think we know much more about its essential nature than F. W. H. Myers knew when writing at the beginning of the century.[2] It appears that extra-sensory faculty is sometimes exercised under hypnosis, and I am inclined to think that this may be due to some degree of astral projection—even though small. It is interesting to notice that Jacob Boehme, on one occasion, passed into a trance through gazing at a burnished pewter dish. He then found that he could "look into the principles and deepest foundations of things". A similar experience is recorded of St. Ignatius Loyola, who, while gazing at running water, entered into an experience in which he could "understand and comprehend spiritual things . . . and this with such clearness that for him all these things were made new".[3] With persons of the quality of Boehme and Loyola the process of withdrawal, which we call trance, freed them not merely to exercise a little extra-sensory perception, but to rise to near-mystical levels.

A mantram is a word or phrase, or a series of sounds, the repetition of which has powerful effects on deeper levels of the mind, and sometimes through these on the environment. The power or influence of a mantram does not reside in any exoteric meaning that words or phrases may possess, but in "the creative thought which ensouls the uttered sound".[4] We had an example of this in Case 3. When a young Indian seeks help on the path of meditation from his guru, he is frequently given a mantram suited to his personal needs. The constant mental repetition of this, perhaps thousands of times a day (called japam), constitutes a method of influencing the deeper mind to help in the reduction of the incessant production of imagery. Such may be called the ritual use of mantrams, and plainsong is probably devised

[1] Muldoon and Carrington, *The Phenomena of Astral Projection* (Rider & Co. Ltd.) An important paper by Dr. J. H. M. Whiteman is found in the Proceedings of the Society for Psychical Research, Vol. 50, p. 240 (May 1956).

[2] *Human Personality and Its Survival of Bodily Death*, Chap. V

[3] Evelyn Underhill, *Mysticism*, p. 58

[4] Arthur Avalon, *The Serpent Power*, Chap. IV (Ganesh & Co., Madras)

to assist in the same way in Western liturgies. The primary function of the mantram is possibly something much more significant than a mere psychological device. I think it may have to do with the linking-up of an individual mind with the creative-destructive source of power—ultimately the imaginal—of which the outer sound was only a gross and feeble manifestation. The reader may turn to the statement on p. 170 about the presuppositions underlying yoga. The idea that the true "name" of a thing is important is strange to Western thought. It frequently occurs in both the Old and New Testaments. A few examples come immediately to mind: the creative power of the Word (Gen. i; John i), the destructive power of ritual sound (Josh. vi), controlling power through knowing a name (Gen. xxxii. 27; Rev. ii. 17), and the well-known cabbalistic tradition that the true name of God can never be spoken.

With these few comments we shall leave the subject of mental techniques for expanding awareness and consider the mind-and-life disciplines.

A discipline differs from a technique in that it is a continuously followed way, and not a particular experimental method. Christianity, Buddhism, Hinduism and most of the world-religions have a current of esoteric discipline which runs like a hidden spring beneath the dry surface of exoteric forms and rituals. If the latter possess any attractiveness or fertility it is because they are sustained and refreshed by the living water. But when the saints and mystics of any religion disappear, that religion dies even though it still counts its members and adherents.

ZEN

Buddhism has always laid stress on the importance of meditation —the journey inwards in pursuit of truth. Most representations of the Buddha show him withdrawn from the sensory world, not merely making journeys of discovery into the vast hidden continent of mind, but penetrating, as we now realise, into regions of essential spirit. Zen Buddhism is a special sect of Chinese Buddhism traced traditionally to the seventh century. It is not a religion: it is a system of mental discipline designed to lead to a higher level of consciousness, for which the Zen term is *satori*. Professor Nukariya's description[1] strongly suggests that *satori* is none other than that stage of the mystic way which has been called Illumination.

[1] D. T. Suzuki, *An Introduction to Zen Buddhism*, p. 10 (Rider & Co. Ltd.)

WATCHER ON THE HILLS

"When we have freed ourselves from the misconception of self we must then awake our inmost pure and godly wisdom. This is what the masters of Zen call the mind of Buddha or Bodhi (the knowledge whereby man experiences Enlightenment or Prajna, the highest wisdom). It is the godly light, the inner heaven, the key to all the treasures of mind, the focal point of thought and consciousness, the source of power and might, the seat of goodness, of justice, of sympathy, of the measure of all things. When this inmost knowledge is fully awakened we are able to understand that each of us is identical in spirit, in being and in nature with universal life, or Buddha, etc."

Observe that here are all the marks of the state of Illumination. The centre of consciring is moved from the limited finite ego to the Spiritual Self. Note the references to the "godly light" and to oneness. It is probably the same experience which St. Paul[1] described in the words: "I live, and yet no longer I, but Christ liveth in me." Dr. C. G. Jung, in a foreword to Dr. Suzuki's book, agrees that the achievement of *satori* is mystical experience, but as we have previously indicated, we differ from him in the interpretation of mysticism. To him it is a state of psychological wholeness achieved by the integration of unconscious with conscious mind—the so-called process of individuation. To us there is a vast difference between the Enlightened being and the psychologically "whole" being. The former state involves a much higher integration, namely of the centre of consciring, ego, or soul, with the Spirit (which is beyond mind). This of course results in the disappearance of "I-ness" in opposition to "other-ness".

Suzuki's exposition of Zen insights is one which Western mystics would find no difficulty in accepting. He insists that inner realisation is all that matters: that all teachings, expositions and formulations in words are valueless. He insists that Zen is extremely simple: it is just living with this inner light. It is pure experience, in which the self and the not-self, subject and object, are not separated by a barrier. Since the reasoning mind necessarily makes these distinctions (for it cannot function otherwise), the technique of Zen appears to be one of attrition of the logical mind. It seeks to get behind the mind with its logic to an insight which transcends them, and which Suzuki describes as "the perception of Reality itself". Because this is the aim, most of the recorded conversations of Zen masters with their students sound complete nonsense to our ears. The process is one of debunking logic. One example of this may suffice.[2]

[1] Gal. ii. 20   [2] *loc. cit.*, p. 57

168

A philosopher-pupil addresses the Master:

"'With what frame of mind should one discipline oneself in the truth?'

"Said the Zen Master, 'There is no mind to be framed, nor is there any truth in which to be disciplined.'

" 'If there is no mind to be framed and no truth in which to be disciplined, why do you have a daily gathering of monks who are studying Zen and disciplining themselves in the truth?'

"The Master replied, 'I have not an inch of space to spare, and where could I have a gathering of monks? I have no tongue, and how would it be possible for me to advise others to come to me?'

"The philosopher then exclaimed, 'How can you tell me a lie like that to my face?'

" 'When I have no tongue to advise others, is it possible for me to tell a lie?'

"Said Doko despairingly, 'I cannot follow your reason.'

" 'Neither do I understand myself,' concluded the Zen Master."

Zen texts are full of this kind of inconsequential talk which clearly contains nothing of value. I have not come across any suggestion except one of Dr. Jung's,[1] as to *how* this kind of dialectic assists the participant to pass beyond logic and duality. Perhaps in the mind which tries to regard it logically there is produced a kind of exhaustion or "drugging" which has analogues in those physical methods which seek to exhaust or drug the brain. I think Dr. Jung would agree so far. He believes, however, that with the cessation of the image-making faculty this energy of the conscious mind then becomes available to the unconscious mind and ultimately builds up to a point of permitting a break-through of contents of the personal unconscious into consciousness. On his view, when a proper adjustment is made to this invasion there is achieved completeness, wholeness and integration. My view is, rather, that if this happens it is a phenomenon quite distinct from mystical experience or *satori*. I suggest that with the cessation of the image-making faculty and quiescence of the conscious mind, the centre of consciring need no longer attend to this level, and is free to be drawn upwards to a union or near-union with the Spirit.

RAJA YOGA

This is the science and technique of exploring the mind—not other peoples' minds, but one's own. It originated in, and is maintained in, India, where it is traced back some two millennia to the

[1] *Introduction to Zen Buddhism*, p. 22

Sutras of Patanjali. Concerning the meanings of these *Sutras* many books have been written.[1] The idea is that by diligent practice the usual constant activity of the mind can be checked. The mind's attention has first to be effectively detached from all sensory impressions. The flow of internal imagery has next to be stopped, and, finally, the attention is (so to speak) turned inwards to make possible a study of the heights and depths of mind itself. It is primarily an occult way rather than a mystical one, for the aim is knowledge and understanding. The pre-supposition of yoga is that the gross external world is but the manifestation of a finer internal world, and that by learning to understand the latter, the former is brought under control. Matter and mind are recognised as manifestations, differing only in degree, of the basic world-stuff called *prakriti*. The other fundamental element in the world (in this dualistic philosophy) is the immaterial *purusha* which observes. These terms correspond fairly closely to our own terms "conscita" and "consciring".

It is impossible to condense into a few sentences the techniques which are used in yoga, to which years of assiduous practice usually need to be devoted to secure results. Unusual breathing rhythms are adopted to stimulate psychic centres within the body. Vivekananda[2] describes the principal steps as follows:

"If the mind can first concentrate upon an object, and then is able to continue in that concentration for a length of time, and then by continued concentration to dwell only on the internal part of the perception of which the object was the effect, everything comes under the control of such a mind. This meditative state is the highest state of existence."

I do not see any good reason to doubt that there are, in the remoter parts of India and Tibet, adepts in these practices who have developed what we in the West would regard as miraculous powers. The evidence of Western para-psychology shows that such powers do exist. In one form or another, yoga is the instrument of occultism. The yogi who proceeds to the frontier of the mind's powers discovers, however, something of another order. I shall quote Vivekananda again.[3]

"There is a still higher plane upon which the mind can work. It can go beyond consciousness. Just as unconscious work is beneath consciousness so there is another work which is above consciousness, and which

[1] e.g. Prabhavananda and Isherwood, *How to Know God* (George Allen and Unwin Ltd., 1953)
[2] *The Complete Works of Vivekananda*, Vol. I, p. 186
[3] *loc. cit.*, p. 180

also is not accompanied with the feeling of egoism. The feeling of egoism is only on the middle plane. When the mind is above or below that line there is no feeling of 'I' and yet the mind works."

I should express these observations differently—for nothing in my view can go beyond consciousness, which is an ultimate. But the reader will clearly appreciate that in these terms the Swami is trying to convey the fact of higher levels on which mystical experience occurs.

THE MYSTIC WAY

The life-long disciplines of the great Christian mystics cannot easily be summarised. I shall quote below a few phrases and sentences of Evelyn Underhill[1] to indicate briefly the methods used.

"This strange art of contemplation, which the mystic tends to practise during the whole of his career—which develops step by step with his vision and his love—demands of the self which undertakes it the same hard dull work, the same slow training of the will, which lies behind all supreme achievement." (p. 307)

"This entails a concentration, a turning inwards of those faculties which the normal self has been accustomed to turn outwards, and fritter upon the manifold illusions of daily life. It means, during the hours of introversion, a retreat from and a refusal of the Many, in order that the mind may be able to apprehend the One." (p. 307)

The process of spiritual growth has been described in terms of three successive techniques called Recollection, Quiet and Contemplation. The first method is associated with purification of the self, the second method is characteristic of Illumination, and the third is used by those near to, or living, the Unitive Life.

Recollection is the same as one-pointed concentration on a word, image or idea.

"The self, concentrated upon this image or idea, dwelling on it more than thinking about it—as one may gaze upon a picture that one loves—falls gradually and insensibly into the condition of reverie . . . To one in whom this state is established, consciousness seems like a blank field, save for the one point in its centre, the subject of the meditation. Towards this focus the introversive self seems to press inwards from every side; still faintly conscious of the buzz of the external world outside its ramparts, but refusing to respond to its appeals. Presently the subject of meditation

[1] Evelyn Underhill, *Mysticism* (Methuen & Co. Ltd., 1949 Ed.)

begins to take on a new significance; to glow with life and light. The
contemplative suddenly feels that he knows it, in the complete, vital,
but indescribable way in which one knows a friend. More, through it
hints are coming to him of mightier, nameless things. It ceases to be a
picture and becomes a window . . ." (pp. 314-5)

This method of discipline is more valuable as a training than for
its results: it is a bringing of the unruly, restless mind under control.

The next method or technique, called Quiet, is where the image
or idea is inhibited and thought entirely ceases. "The strange silence
which is the outstanding quality of this state", says Evelyn Underhill,
"is not describable". "Nothing but the paramount fact of his own
existence remains."

"He is there, as it were poised, resting, waiting he does not know for
what; only he is conscious that all, even in this utter emptiness, is well.
Presently, however, he becomes aware that *Something* fills this emptiness;
something omnipresent, intangible, like sunny air . . . he begins to notice
That which has always been within." (p. 318)

The experience of this phase is said to be "possible of attainment
by all those who have sufficiently disciplined themselves in patience,
recollection, and humility". This phase is described as presenting
spiritual dangers, in that some have continued in it indefinitely in a
condition of unproductive passivity or "Quietism" instead of
continuing to aspire humbly to God.

Of the third phase, or method of Contemplation, Evelyn
Underhill says:

"It is to transcend alike the stages of symbol and of silence; and
energise enthusiastically on those high levels which are dark to the
intellect but radiant to the heart." (p. 328)

It is said to be a supreme power of knowing in which knowing
and being are inseparable. As Delacroix said, "These two things tend
at bottom to become one. The mystic has more and more the
impression of being that which he knows, and of knowing that which
he is." In this activity all our faculties of thinking, feeling, perception
and loving, are merged into a unity. Of this kind of knowing-being
Evelyn Underhill says:

"Instead of sharply perceiving the fragment, we apprehend, yet how
we know not, the solemn presence of the whole." (p. 330)

"There is no certitude to equal the mystic's certitude: no impotence more complete than that which falls on those who try to communicate it." (p. 331)

Contemplation is said to be (unlike the two previous phases), "a general name for a large group of states, partly governed—like all other forms of mystical activity—by the temperament of the subject". Two things are emphasised however: (1) In Contemplation there is an experience of the All, not as in meditation, of a part or an aspect. Moreover, it is "given rather than attained". (2) The apprehension is "by participation, not by way of observation". Says Evelyn Underhill:

"The contemplative self who has attained this strange country can only tell an astonished and incredulous world that here his greatest deprivation is also his greatest joy; that here the extremes of possession and surrender are the same, that ignorance and knowledge, light and dark are One. Love has led him into that timeless, spaceless world of Being which is the peaceful ground, not only of the individual striving spirit, but also of the striving universe; and he can but cry with Philip, 'It is enough'." (p. 339)

It is scarcely necessary to draw attention to the fact that all these ways, whether Christian, Buddhist or Hindu, have much in common. It could not be otherwise if they are all approaches to Reality. Where they differ from all other methods of expanding awareness is that they represent *permanent spiritual achievement*, not a temporarily wider apprehension, however impressive.

It is perhaps appropriate to recall what Ruysbroeck said of the mystical heights:

"And none can arrive there by knowledge or subtlety, nor by any exercises: but he whom God wills to unite to His own Spirit and to illuminate by Himself, can contemplate God."

Chapter

II

MYSTICISM AND LIFE

O Thou,
God of all long desirous roaming,
Our hearts are sick of fruitless homing,
And crying after lost desire.
Hearten us onward! as with fire
Consuming dreams of other bliss.
The best Thou givest, giving this
Sufficient thing—to travel still
Over the plain, beyond the hill,
Unhesitating through the shade,
Amid the silence unafraid,
Till, at some sudden turn, one sees
Against the black and muttering trees
Thine altar, wonderfully white,
Among the Forests of the Night.
RUPERT BROOKE (*The Song of the Pilgrims*)

"THERE is a tale that a man inspired by God once went out from the creaturely realms into the vast waste. There he wandered till he came to the gates of the mystery. He knocked. From within came the cry: 'What do you want here?' He said, 'I have proclaimed your praise in the ears of mortals, but they were deaf to me. So I come to you that you yourself may hear me and reply.' 'Turn back,' came the cry from within. 'Here is no ear for you. I have sunk my hearing in the deafness of mortals.' "[1]

This parable of Martin Buber is a reminder that the flight to God from the works of God is no compliment to the Creator. That which a watcher sees on the hills he must relate to life in the valleys. In this concluding chapter I propose to write, first, of the relevance of the mystical view of life to our present situation, and, secondly, of its importance to the ordinary person concerned with the daily struggle to live worthily.

THE PRESENT SITUATION

It is a platitude to say that civilisation has reached a critical phase. All human living, whether it conforms to a pattern called "civilised" or not, is based on assumptions. These assumptions are

[1] Martin Buber, *Between Man and Man* (Routledge & Kegan Paul Ltd., 1947)

174

extremely powerful and they are seldom examined. Some of the basic ones probably never change, while others, which we may describe as working assumptions, change imperceptibly and gradually in the course of a few generations. One of the last group which interests us particularly may be called the assumption of materialism. Its powerful sway over the minds of men has been largely associated with, and caused by, the growth of science and technology. We may summarise it as the belief that the world which our senses disclose is the only real world; that to believe otherwise is mere superstition. From such belief it follows that man's achievements are necessarily bound up with the race—not with the individual who must perish. It follows, moreover, that increased scientific knowledge and mastery of Nature are regarded as the measure of man's progress towards what may vaguely be pictured as an earthly Utopia. Materialists, however, are never very clear about goals. If technology and automation produce a civilisation where there is no economic want, and where the essential labour can be carried out in a few hours out of the twenty-four, presumably men and women will devote themselves to art and philosophy, or to physical enjoyment and the breaking of records, according to their inclination. The goal is perhaps left vague because of the uncertainties inherent in human nature which may close human history at an earlier stage, and also because it is a discouraging thought that a heat-death or a cosmic frost will close it finally in any case. Materialism therefore, makes for living in the present: there is no great incentive to look far ahead.

The modern concern arises, however, because of an immediate menace and not because of distant possibilities. Most thoughtful people agree that the menace exists because the moral progress of the Western world has not kept pace with its scientific achievement. As to why this is the case, opinions may differ. I blame materialism—a fallacious outlook which has grown up gradually, and gathered strength until it has come to occupy the whole background of assumptions upon which our civilisation bases its present actions and its future hopes. The exponents of science and the custodians of religion are, in my opinion, both to blame.

The Churches, which in the West are the custodians of religion, must accept a considerable share of responsibility. To many of us it is evident that they have largely ceased to speak with *first-hand* knowledge of eternal verities. A great organisation has grown up, expensive to maintain and adapted to our civilised life. Spiritual vitality has become a frail and slender thing. Preoccupied with the organisation and things of secondary and even minor importance, the Churches convey no impression of possessing immediate experience of ultimate things, but rather that they are handing on traditions which they have received. This handing-on is all too often in language which seems remote from modern life and is meaningless to modern man. A wise and able psychiatrist, not at all unsympathetic to religion, wrote to me as follows: "Much of what is presented to men as food for the soul is just repetitious nonsense—made worse by the enormous effort which has been put into it—for frivolous light-hearted nonsense is preferable to this heavy-handed stuff. So many of the 'great' religious controversies are no more than words about words about words. Yet words for which blood has been spilled and abominable things have been done . . . Nothing is more tedious and silly than the religious disagreements about wholly unimportant matters. It shows how deep is the human need and how great the longing, that, in spite of this, men and women are still deeply interested and crave for truth. This is the great miracle of the Churches."

The cleavage between the scientific and the religious attitudes is wide, but not fundamental. The scientists' own approach to truth has been experimental and verifiable by all who could carry out the experiments. They have assumed that religious truth was unverifiable —necessarily a matter of faith, and therefore quite possibly illusory. These assumptions are not justified, and at this point scientists are blameworthy. Their suspicions have, however, tended to be strengthened rather than dispelled when the defence of religion has been made in tones of authority rather than through the testimony of the mystic. For one might call the mystic the scientist of ultimate things; he is himself both the observer and the instrument. It is he who has verified in his experience that the *basic* data of religion are trustworthy: that God *is*, that He is infinitely beyond us and yet infinitely near, that He is Love and Beauty, Wisdom and Goodness—Perfection's own unutterable Self. All the great mystics have verified these things for themselves: but do not let us suppose that there is any quick and easy way to their experience. Why should there be? This is the pearl of great price which demands for its possession all that a man has. No man can sit down and produce a masterpiece of Art, when he wills. He can prepare himself for the possibility of doing so by a long and diligent apprenticeship to the discipline of his craft. Through great devotion he can acquire skill and master his medium, so that when the moment of inspiration comes he may recognise it, capture it and preserve it for ever. Should we expect high mystical experience to come easily, when the soul has itself to become the prepared instrument?

It is extremely important for our modern age that the gulf between the scientific and religious outlooks should be bridged. Many leading scientists who are acquainted with philosophy already recognise that materialism as an outlook is hopeless. But it certainly does not follow from this that religion as it is presented today will win their allegiance. I believe, however, that the first-hand experience of the mystics is testimony which should appeal to them as offering evidence of the existence of high levels of Reality (which have been, and can be, reached), which are the source of sustenance of the essence of religion.

I have stated that first-hand confirmation of the mystic's experience is not something that can be lightly offered or rapidly undertaken: the will cannot command it. It does, however, now seem possible to offer the scientist a drug-induced experience which may disclose to him certain things. Among these are the existence of levels of Reality other than the physical, and the ability of mind to function in a manner, and with powers which are not derived from nor dependent upon the sensory-brain mechanism. If scientists come to recognise even so much as this, materialism is dead and gone for ever, for the sensory-brain picture of reality is *experienced* as only a limited aspect of a greater whole. The way is then open for the scientist, *as a man*, to regard what the mystic or religious genius tries to convey through the limited medium of words as a form of genuine experience on still higher levels of the world. This is one of the most exciting prospects which lies before us: that alert, intelligent scientific thinkers, whose concern is with truth, can be offered a glimpse behind the curtain which has hitherto obscured the distance. The danger is that they will then transfer the spirit of dogmatic materialism on to a new level and fail to look further into those more distant regions in which man is himself the instrument of his own discovery.

THE VALIDITY OF MYSTICAL EXPERIENCE

It is a good thing to bring the mind's critical faculty to bear upon every experience of life, as long as we do not regard reason as the sole arbiter of truth. Nowhere is this more important than in religion where the demand for "faith" is so often made in the wrong place. I recall a compliment which Isherwood paid to Swami Vivekananda —"He brought to his religious life that most valuable quality, intelligent doubt." The religious outlook held by a man who has faced, and continues to face, his doubts is a great deal more worth having than that of the man who has repressed them. *In most religions the ultimate verities are believed—and may therefore be doubted; in mysticism they are experienced, and doubt is no longer possible.*

In an unpublished prose account[1] of an out-of-the-body experience, Mr. J. Redwood-Anderson has described a symbolical vision of the soul's progress which was presented to him. It was a drama in which he seemed to participate with ecstatic joy. Writing of it he says:

"Whatever this experience, this adventure, may have been—vision or some super-dream or very actuality (and now I speak of the ecstasy of that final self-transforming ascent)—that ecstasy was *a felt experience*, and therefore pre-eminently *real*—for an unreal feeling is a contradiction in terms. And this means that somewhere in the Universe, either without us or within, that joy and the Source of that joy abide: somewhere, beyond all the pain, frustration and contradiction of this or any other imaginable world, there exists awaiting the soul that inexpressible apotheosis of being . . . This feeling, this ecstasy, I say, whatever may be said of the rest, *must be real* since I have felt it, and, by that fact, if no other, conferred upon it its title to ultimate truth."

Does conviction based upon deep feeling point infallibly to truth? It is a question of great importance, for mystical states are usually characterised by outstanding feeling-quality. Some mystical states appear to embrace greatly widened knowledge, but this is seldom available as a criterion for judgment since either the language in which to express the knowledge is unavailable, or the technical skill to interpret what is apprehended is not part of the mystic's equipment. The critic of conviction-based-on-feeling has a strong case to be answered. He points out that since feelings are not communicable (in a generally accepted sense), they can have authority only for the person who enjoys them. Moreover, he will say, some people have convictions not based upon reason and therefore presumably based upon feeling, of the most absurd and generally unacceptable kind. For example, Mr. Custance tells us[2] that in the depressive phase of his psychosis two plain enamelled iron wall-brackets in his bathroom became "figures of appalling horror" whom he named subsequently Satan and Beelzebub. But psychosis apart, when we con-

[1] Entitled *The Third World*
[2] *Adventures into the Unconscious*, p. 55

sider the queer convictions based on feeling of a great variety of religious people with strange unshakable ideas, what weight can be attached to feelings as pointers to truth?

It is characteristic of feeling-states that they are not originated on conscious levels of the mind by the will. They have their origin on other levels where they may be of great strength, as in acute depression, or with "falling in love", and they may defy all conscious efforts to eliminate them. Impermeability to reason is no criterion of reliability or unreliability, of falsity or of truth. When we recognise different levels of Reality we face the obvious possibility that convictions based on feeling may rise into consciousness from such levels. On the one hand, we may expect to find obsessions and superstitions from the "unconscious", and on the other hand we may find poetic insights and intuitions from higher levels. If there are reliable criteria for discrimination they are of the greatest importance to us in weighing the testimony of the mystics.

It is perhaps necessary to point out that the word "feeling" is used very loosely in our daily speech. It is often wrongly used as when a person says, "I *feel* that you have misunderstood my question." For "feel" should be substituted "think". Consider the three statements: "I feel cold", "I feel angry", "I feel inspired". The first is a statement based on physical sensation, the second is based upon emotion, the third is based upon intuition. None of these things can be commanded by the will—and this is what they have in common— but observe that they are very different sorts of "feeling" and come from different levels of the self. It is generally only of the third sort of feeling that we are concerned to ask: does it, when strongly held, point us to truth?

I think there are three criteria which, where they can be answered in the affirmative, offer a sound (even though not an infallible) indication of this.

(1) The pragmatic test. Has it led to well-balanced, happy, serene living of an enhanced quality?

(2) Is it *consistent* with the well-established findings of reason? (This need not imply that it is *supported* by reason.)

(3) Is it unifying and integrative, or isolating and destructive so far as the individual's relationship to an all-embracing whole is concerned?

It is obvious that all psychotic products resulting in obsessional feeling-states cannot pass the first criterion. It is clear that all allegedly religious people who, as a friend of mine once said, "have only intolerance in common, and are sure that if only people believed as they do, all would we well", are ruled out by the third criterion.

If the reader will turn again to the accounts of mystical experience presented in Chapters 3 to 6, he will find that affirmative answers to the above criteria can usually be given. I quote from some further accounts of mystical experience[1] where the experients are summarising the effect it had on their life. Consider them in the light of the above criteria.

"I was dazed but at the same time thrilled with the ecstasy of it. It was a 'joy unspeakable and full of glory'. I seemed to be walking on air; the whole world was changed; everything was brighter than it had been before, even on that bright morning, and was alive with a deep, calm, radiant and joyful life. I was filled with happiness and peace, and knew intuitively that I had found the Reality for which I had sought . . . I was amazed too at my understanding of things. It seemed as if my mind had but to present a matter to my consciousness for it to be understood fully and completely. After I had diarised my rough notes of the experience I worked at a lecture which I was due to deliver that evening. I was amazed at the wider understanding that had so strangely come to me, but I did not realise until quite long afterwards how completely my outlook on life, and in fact my whole scheme of things had been changed. Nor did I foresee that I would speak for years afterwards on the understanding that came to me in that brief hour's meditation." (pp. 58-59)

He speaks also of the considerably improved physical health, of his widened sympathies, and of the growth of psychic sensitivity, and a sense of conscious immortality.

"Enhancement of spiritual life has certainly followed. I had often doubted before in the face of the world's sorrows and imperfections, but I never doubted after this. It was my first experience of certain *knowledge* of Reality and its Glory. Nothing can ever negate it . . . For the last seven years I have been a voluntary prison-worker; and I am very happy and in better health than ever in youth, notwithstanding narrow means, fatigue, failures, etc. in daily life. I have remained unmarried and I have never regretted it! At the same time I am thankful to say I *have* experienced 'being in love'; and I think this is a much slighter and a transient form of illumination." (p. 83)

"I knew I was not alone—that I could never be alone any more, that the universe beyond held no menace, for I was part of it; that in some way for which I had sought in vain for so many years, I *belonged* and, because I belonged, I was no longer I, but something different which could never

[1] Winslow Hall, M.D., *Recorded Illuminates* (C. W. Daniel Co. Ltd., 1937)

be afraid in the old ways, or cowardly with the old cowardice . . . I am very much the same person to look at. I am just as hopeless in dealing with the mechanism of life as ever I was. I don't suppose that even my friends notice any difference. Nevertheless the difference is there. I have learned to accept. And what I mean by acceptance is this: that my little personality does not matter any more. I am not a whole; I am a part, and when my work is over I shall go. And there is no menace in the immensities any more. Somehow they have me in their keeping, and, stranger still, I them in mine. I bear them up, they me. My isolation and inanition were at an end: suddenly I had become a man with a mission, full of energy and conviction." (p. 108-9)

"To enter today into the subtleties of my own transcendental feelings is beyond my power. But I have a memory which seems to hold in solution all the lesser memories of what passed during that crisis in my inner life; to hold these in solution and in some sort to renew them and to admit them to a share in its own vividness and clarity. Out of all my experiences, justifying them and unifying them, and absorbing them as it were into itself, emerged one triumphant conviction—a conviction which passed far beyond the limits of normal certitude—the conviction that the Universe is an organic, a living Whole: that All is One." (p. 135)

"I was conscious of a feeling of bodily well-being, vigour and lightness, as if I were walking on air; though certainly there was nothing in the way of bodily levitation . . . There was an intense feeling of joy, certainty, union with the All—of 'omni-identity', if the word may be passed. Eternity was present and immortality self-evident. Men and women were as 'gods walking' . . . About a month after my experience I wrote 'God is all, and I am part of God' . . . It is still, more than twenty-three years after its first appearance, energising me ever." (p. 142)

I submit that this kind of testimony strikes an authentic note. If my intuition is wrong at this point, it is, as far as I am concerned, wholly untrustworthy. To compare such feeling-states with delusional states, with the products of auto-suggestion, or with wishes running riot, is like comparing the clear sparkling air of mountain tops with that of foetid slums. The various feeling-states doubtless have this in common, that they are invasions of the conscious field from an extra-liminal region, just as the two kinds of air are doubtless chemically akin. But the qualities they do not share in common are enormously significant in the scale of values.

TO THE ORDINARY PERSON

I have written this book because the testimony of those who have had moments of mystical experience seems to me a clear pointer to the truth about the world. I find these testimonies impressive in their sincerity, in their unanimity, and in their influence on the lives of those to whom they came. It is satisfying to have the assurance that (in William James' words), "the nature of Reality is congenial to powers [and hopes] which we possess". But for every one who has had such a glimpse there are a thousand who would desire it, but have had none. Immersed in the routine and monotony of every-day life, uninspiring and uninspired, they feel remote from such experience.

The great majority of the accounts of mystical experience included in this book are of ordinary people. Many were suffering, anxious, tired people doing the world's commonplace work. They lived in the same world as we do—but in their high moment, *they saw it differently*, and were convinced that they saw it truly. As a result, what did they say of the world which often seems so grey to us?

(1) *Love pervades it.* The hatreds, the misunderstandings, the conflicts and the suffering, seemed to them like waves on the surface of the ocean depths, or as the fog, which obscures the ever-shining sun. "It was", said a worried engineer, "the sense of the presence of an irresistible power wholly and utterly benevolent . . . The certainty of all-pervading and immutable love was so tremendous that I simply went on up the hill completely absorbed in the extraordinary experience" (Case 10). "I was aware of Love—Universal Love—Peace, Joy, Bliss, Ecstasy . . . to such an extent that it is impossible to express it in words" (Case 13). "In this timeless second", said Brother Mandus, "I knew a Love, Knowledge and Ecstasy transcending anything I could understand or describe" (Case 14).

(2) *It is a Unity.* All the loneliness which people feel, all the sense of isolation, of meeting circumstances in single combat, of being the victim of chance events—are wrong impressions. A woman who went through a period of "dreadful alone-ness", became seriously ill, and for weeks wanted to die, describing the timeless moment during her convalescence said, "Barriers were down; my alone-ness had gone; I was at one with every living creature and thing. I *knew* that, despite almost overwhelming evidence to the contrary, a trinity of Truth, Beauty and Justice was the basis of life, and that 'somehow good would be the final goal of ill'. In that beautiful biblical phrase, I *knew* that 'underneath were the Everlasting Arms' " (Case 12). "In some way for which I had sought in vain for so many years, I *belonged* . . . I am not a whole; I am a part . . . And there is no menace in the immensities any more. Somehow they have me

in their keeping—and, stranger still, I them in mine. I bear them up, they me."

The theme runs through these moments of mystical insight, and if this is true, it means that when a person feels separate and lonely he is suffering from a blindness to the truth of things which he should seek to overcome. If we are linked with all others in a great unity, it follows that there must be pattern and purpose to make it a unity. We who look at life from the periphery see only the chaos of a myriad apparently unrelated happenings. The mystic tells us not to be misled, for in the moment when he looked outwards from within, he saw the Divine purpose working slowly onwards to a perfect goal. "I had often doubted before in the face of the world's sorrows and imperfections, but I never doubted after this."

(3) *Perfection underlies the Whole.* When a work of art is being made, whether it be a painting, or a piece of sculpture, or architecture, the state of becoming often seems to deny the possibility of final beauty. Yet the vision is there in the artist's mind, and if for one moment we could share it, we should see the perfect image co-existing with the changing external creation. It is not that one is illusory and the other actual. Both are actual on different levels. We see only one, while the mystic, for a moment, sees both. "None of the pleasures of life, the ecstasy of the poet and musician, nor the creative joy of the mathematican can come within a million miles of the supreme happiness of this mystic event" (Case 10). "Somehow I *knew* that what I had experienced was Reality and that Reality is Perfection . . . What I chiefly remember is the Light and the ecstasy of Perfection being Real". (Case 15)

In his remarkable book[1] R. H. Ward has recounted a mystical experience of his friend A. A. describes himself on one of the crests of a wave of uplifted consciousness:

"I heard vividly, shockingly, and as instantaneously as one might see a flash of lightning, what I can only call an inward voice which said 'There is something perfect.' The phrase conveys nothing of the meaning it bore at that moment, for it had unbelievable depths of significance. The voice seemed to be telling me in those four words everything that it is important and necessary to know. 'There is something perfect' was a summary of what it is to be in the presence of God Who is perfection's Self. Since it is true that 'there is something perfect', all the imperfections to which we are heirs could be seen in their insignificant proportions. These words applied to my sick friend, to her self imprisoned in her sick

[1] *loc. cit.*, p. 201

body, to the trees and the moonlit landscape even, marvellous though they were, for though I saw them now as part of perfection or in their reality, they too, seen as I should see them again next time I walked this lane, would suffer the sickness of being 'of this world'.

"I stood still in the road, filled to the brim with this wonderful and joyful realisation, that whatever we may have to endure of pain, sickness, grief and man's inhumanity to man, *there is still something perfect in all created things, that ultimately they live by it, and that nothing else matters.*"

Love, unbounded Love and Joy pervade the whole; we belong to this great whole and have our small share in its pattern. The underlying pattern is perfect: Beauty's self and Wisdom's self meet, fully know each other, and are fully known. "But", says a toiling, frustrated person, "what does this matter to me if *I* cannot feel it?" The answer is that *nothing else matters*, and that if we humbly offer our co-operation in the plan we can be the means of bringing through into ordinary life a little of this Reality. It all depends on how we look at life.

Julia de Beausobre[1] tells of her detention in an inner prison of the O.G.P.U. and of an interview with the governor of the prison:

"There is only a corner of the table between us. We look at each other. And we see each other. In that moment's hush that follows we are present at the eternal miracle, the lightning-quick nativity of human understanding. I see that it is not only Party discipline that keeps this old and saddened Communist from giving up the distasteful work to which he has been appointed. I see that in the unavowed depths of his heart, in the subconscious luminous clarity of it, he knows that it is good and right for him to be Governor of this Palace of Torture, instead of the awful freaks who might be if he were not. I see him realise with wonder and relief that I am not hostile to him or to anyone or anything. The barrier of cruel superficialities has fallen away, and we both know that all things in all eternity will be good and clear between us. If only—*we do not forget.*

"And because miracles are sacred and must be veiled, he repeats: 'Any requests?' And I say: 'I forgot to take my sponge with me when I was brought here. Might I have a sponge?' "

All redemption of the lower levels depends upon bringing down into them something from higher levels, and this can only be done through the willingness of those who offer sacrificial service. Some

---

[1] Julia de Beausobre, *The Woman Who Could Not Die* (Chatto & Windus Ltd.)

gleams of the Joy of Reality can be brought through by those who serve cheerfully in humble and menial tasks, by those who show courage and serenity when suffering, by those who maintain a radiation of happy humour in a difficult situation, and by those who distribute a little light-heartedness when the general atmosphere is one of friction or gloom. All this is redemptive work.

Few of the custodians of religion in either East or West have ever made it sufficiently clear that the quality of joy, when expressed in ordinary life, is of the highest spiritual value, and as a habit is a cardinal virtue. There is no evidence that Christ was a man of sorrows except to the extent that he entered into the sorrows of other people in order to lift them out of their despair. A man who turned water into wine at a marriage feast, who drew attention to the lilies of the field "how they grow" as a pattern for anxious men, and who took a child as an exemplar of many qualities which His followers would do well to emulate, must have had about Him an essential radiation of Joy. St. Paul, who might have had just occasion for concern, constantly exhorted his friends to "Rejoice". It has been a complete and utter travesty of Christ's teaching to find organisations of His self-styled followers fearful about their own salvation and steeped in Calvinistic gloom. It has been a wicked denial of all that Christ stands for, when some so-called "priests" have used the threat of eternal damnation to endeavour to secure conformity to their beliefs and practice.

The mystics tell us of Divine Love and Joy pervading the whole of existence, and ordinary folk can help it to appear through them even in the midst of tragedy, by showing courage and love. "The religion that can bring back a capacity for joy into the life of man will be a live and holy religion" writes a friend of mine.

Consider Beauty: those who look for it will find it everywhere. In spite of all that man has done to flaunt the crude and ugly, the miracles of Nature are widespread for those who remain constantly aware. Even the flower in a window-box in a grubby street will speak of the Joy and Beauty at the heart of Creation. The Irish poet A. E. was particularly sensitive to this and wrote[1]

> In that wild orchid that your feet
> In their next falling shall destroy
> Minute and passionate and sweet
> The Might Master holds His joy.

[1] 'Continuity': *Collected Poems of A. E.* (Macmillan & Co. Ltd.)

Though the crushed jewels droop and fade
The Artist's labours will not cease,
And of the ruins shall be made
Some yet more lovely masterpiece.

If this can be said of the wild orchid, how much more can it be said of human lives crushed by the feet of circumstance. I am led to make this concluding remark. The soul of man is never crushed: it rests inviolate above the stresses of life. Only the personality may suffer a sense of restriction, suffering and futility. It need not do so if it could fully realise that it is only the surface of being that presents these aspects, and that its own part is fully and faithfully accomplished if by a cheerful and undaunted reaction to these aspects it offers spiritual treasure to the soul.

I have just quoted A. E., and perhaps I may quote his friend W. B. Yeats[1] who, rightly understood, says all that I am trying to say:

I will arise and go now, for always night and day
I hear lake water lapping with low sounds by the shore;
While I stand on the roadway, or on the pavements gray,
I hear it in the deep heart's core.

How sad never to hear it!

[1] 'The Lake Isle of Innisfree', *Collected Poems of W. B. Yeats* (Macmillan & Co. Ltd.)

INDEX